"Wonderfully authentic. Maura Matarese has written a book that emphasizes the importance of the Socratic message with all the excitement and drama of opening day at Fenway Park. If you read this book, you will feel that the game of love, loss, and courage is definitely worth playing."

- James J. Lynch, PhD, author of *The Broken Heart: The Medical Consequences of Loneliness* and *A Cry Unheard: New Insights into the Medical Consequences of Loneliness.*

"A terrific book. Maura Matarese shows us how psychotherapy is not for the faint of heart, yet no matter what the crisis, there's always hope."

- Mark J. Albanese, MD, author of *Understanding Addiction as Self Medication: Finding Hope Beneath the Pain.*

Finding

HOPE

in the Crisis

A THERAPIST'S PERSPECTIVE ON
LOVE, LOSS, AND COURAGE

Maura A. Matarese, MA, LMHC

BALBOA.
PRESS

A DIVISION OF HAY HOUSE

Balboa Press books may be ordered through booksellers or by contacting:

Balboa Press
A Division of Hay House
1663 Liberty Drive
Bloomington, IN 47403
www.balboapress.com
1 (877) 407-4847

Because of the dynamic nature of the Internet, any web addresses or links contained in this book may have changed since publication and may no longer be valid. The views expressed in this work are solely those of the author and do not necessarily reflect the views of the publisher, and the publisher hereby disclaims any responsibility for them.

The author of this book does not dispense medical advice or prescribe the use of any technique as a form of treatment for physical, emotional, or medical problems without the advice of a physician, either directly or indirectly. The intent of the author is only to offer information of a general nature to help you in your quest for emotional and spiritual well-being. In the event you use any of the information in this book for yourself, which is your constitutional right, the author and the publisher assume no responsibility for your actions.

Print information available on the last page.

ISBN: 978-1-9822-0442-6 (sc)
ISBN: 978-1-9822-0443-3 (hc)
ISBN: 978-1-9822-0450-1 (e)

Library of Congress Control Number: 2018905834

Balboa Press rev. date: 08/03/2018

CONTENTS

PART 1
The Crisis: When Love's Labor Is Lost

PART 2
Finding Hope: The Road Back Home

PART 3
Courage and Creative Solutions: The Road to Love's Labor's Won

ACKNOWLEDGMENTS

I wish to thank and acknowledge the following people:

First and foremost, my family: Dad, John, and my mother, who left us too soon. My creative well springs from you all.

To my dearest of friends: Margaret Latawiec, Marilyn Unger-Riepe, and Amy Johnson; you've been there for me through thick and thin. I am blessed to have you in my life.

To my consultants and therapists, present and past: Fran Booth, Bob Fox, Nancy Costikyan, Jane Cole, Ronni Kotler, and Marc Albanese; your wisdom and care has nurtured my talent and very being. This book would not have happened without your attunement, advice, and encouragement throughout the years.

To my IFS consulting group and the IFS community: your unwavering commitment to accessing Self-energy has kept me on the path to do the same.

To Maria Martin at Forever Slender Med Spa in Wayland, Massachusetts.

To Angela Pennington, whose gift of Jyotish has always helped me see if and when the stars would align.

To Frogs, Ferris wheels, rhinestones, and roses.

To Randall Forsythe, whose genius always sparks my curiosity and inspires me.

To fools who dare to dream and those with the courage to free themselves to be themselves, I bow to you.

Om Gam Gannapataye Namaha (Ganesh prayer for removing obstacles).

FOREWORD

James J. Lynch, PhD

It was my rare privilege to spend my academic career at the Johns Hopkins University Medical School, the University of Pennsylvania Medical School, and finally as professor of psychiatry at the University of Maryland Medical School, delineating the many major feeder streams that contribute to the ever-growing lethality of human loneliness in our culture. In a research journey that spanned over three decades, it became obvious that human beings can indeed die of a *Broken Heart* (Basic Books, 1977). Indeed, as the medical data revealed, the concept of a broken heart was far more than a romantic metaphor; it was an overwhelming medical reality. Only gradually did we come to understand why and how human loneliness had emerged as one of the hidden, albeit leading causes of premature death in America. Indeed, patients suffering from cardiovascular disease frequently increased their blood pressure far more dramatically during human dialogue than they did after maximal exercise. There was a profound, albeit hidden *Language of the Heart* (Basic Books, 1985) that needed to be understood in order to help patients adopt more effective and authentic ways of communicating. Authenticity had to be restored to dialogue that frequently had been shattered in childhood.

In the course of treating patients for the past forty years, I've tried to address the issue of authenticity in therapy straight away by asking each patient at the outset of therapy whether they thought they could share with me any feeling that I've never felt. At first, such a question usually elicits confusion and needs to be asked once again: "If I have never felt sadness, do you think you could share your sadness with me?" Not wishing to prolong this line of questioning in a cat-and-mouse fashion, I would usually quickly add, "Then you should hope that I have suffered as much as you have, perhaps in different ways, but sufficient to help us share similar feelings in therapy."

Authenticity is the central clinical message that permeates Maura Matarese's new book, *Finding Hope in the Crisis: A Therapist's Perspective on Love, Loss, and Courage.*

Maura is wonderfully authentic. She shares with the reader her own thoughts and feelings that have been based on her own extraordinary journey. After completing college, she first began her career working as a production assistant in sports television in the competitive Boston marketplace. It was a world where interest in sports has been elevated into the lofty atmosphere of a new type of religion. Yet she is forced to confront the reality that this is a career path largely sealed off from women. Unrecognized at the time, she would come to see this feminine battle as one that can covertly stymie therapeutic relationships.

After seven years in sports broadcasting, Maura then sought meaning in a completely different field of endeavor when she decided to become an actress, working at the Boston Playwrights Theatre, among other Boston-based theater companies. Here, she was exposed to the far deeper meaning of Shakespearean and Greek tragedy. The wisdom of the Greeks would be a theme that began to blossom in her subsequent career as a psychotherapist. Slowly but surely, the very meaning of the word *personality,* which owes its origins to the Greek word *persona* (the mask that actors wore in Greek tragedies), suggests a hiding of their real selves, both from their audiences as well as from themselves. Persona or mask would come to be understood by Maura as the great battle in therapy, as she struggled with herself and with her patients to break down the false sense of self that controls our lives, which eventually must give way to a true sense of self, and the source of hope.

After an acting career, which she loved, Maura then decided to seek a master's degree in clinical mental health counseling. As part of her training and growth, Maura worked in a methadone clinic for the next nine years, both treating patients and supervising clinicians and interns, which brought her even closer to the concept of genuine authenticity as a psychotherapist.

This book is a delightful summary of the various schools of psychoanalytic and depth psychology that have become an integral part of her own pursuit of authenticity in therapy.

One additional note to add to authenticity: I vividly remember holding Maura's hand many, many years ago, as I would take her and my three children to a local candy store in suburban Boston on warm summer's evenings. We always called her "M&M" (Maura Matarese). She was as sweet then as she is today. Although I'm her uncle, I still believe that I can be objective in asserting that she's written a book that contains all the drama of Opening Day at Fenway Park. For some, it will help them to hit a home run at the very beginning of therapy; for others, the ball may dribble past first base and the pennant is lost. If you read this book you will feel that the game is definitely worth playing. In any case, there's always next year.

Shortly before his death, Socrates was put on trial on the charge of "subverting Athenian youth." He famously responded by asserting that "a life unexamined is not a life worth living."

Maura has written a book that emphasizes the importance of the Socratic message. Her goal is to tear down the false images that prevent us from discovering our authentic selves. It involves a therapeutic journey that truly makes life worth living.

PREFACE

What does it mean to be alive?
How are we to act?
What must I do?
—Tina Packer, *Theater, Therapy, and Theology*

"You are closer than you think," my longtime friend and colleague once said to me.

I had been working on a book for several years, though the subject matter kept changing. What first started as *Let the Stars Align: How the Ancient Wisdom of Yoga in Clinical Psychology Can Turn Your Karma into Dharma* then changed to *Understanding Narcissistic and Manipulative Partners at Home and at Work* and then morphed into a new book called *When Someone Wants to Leave.* I now had three book ideas that I had started, with little inspiration to finish any of them. I would start and stop and start and stop again. Words simply wouldn't come to me, and my ideas just didn't gel. Having the classic symptoms of writer's block, including procrastination, depression, and anxiety, left me feeling confused, exhausted, and a bit like a fraud. I knew that I had great ideas but couldn't seem to manifest a whole book out of one in particular.

While struggling to find the energy to work on each book, I somehow found the energy to write a blog, inspired mostly by my clients, who were struggling with their relationships. It sparked my imagination. I had a need to tell the story in my mind's eye, which was why I was writing a book; it just wasn't happening in a linear way.

I am, at heart, a storyteller, a tangential one, though, I must admit.

Great stories, whether we read them or see them on film or in the theater, inspire us to dig deep into our souls and connect to the essence of who we are, which in turn helps us to become who we are meant to be. Believe it or not, everyday, ordinary life is filled with epic stories if we open our eyes, ears, and hearts to experience them. As a psychotherapist, I have had the privilege of doing this on a daily basis. So before I finish telling you the story of how this book came into being, first, let me tell you a bit about my story.

In college, I majored in communications and took a lot of acting classes, which was my true passion. I had a practical side, however, with an affinity for sports, which helped me land my first professional job working as a production assistant in sports television. I spent seven years there, working long hours for little pay, and I got to be part of an exciting world that many longed to be in. In Boston, the sports world has a Hollywood status that many a young, wide-eyed twentysomething professional can easily get caught up it. The epic comebacks and tragic overtime losses of Bruins and Red Sox games, along with working on creative and off-the-wall sports features, captured my attention for a while.

There was also a dark side to it all, especially for a woman, as working in sports was still considered unorthodox back in 1992. We weren't always treated well. Sometimes, false assumptions were made about our motives for choosing this line of work, which were often conveyed in an unmerciful fashion. Some would be touched inappropriately and then threated if they ever considered complaining, and some would have to incur the wrath of their superior's rage (though this was not uncommon for both women and men alike in the broadcast industry). In time, many of us, myself included, became disillusioned with it all.

In spite of this disillusionment, it wasn't easy to leave. Though deep down, I knew that sports television wasn't really my life's passion, it took a while for me to admit this to myself and then find the courage to pursue what was. I had to get really unhappy before I did. It wasn't until I saw how neglectful I had become at work, showing up late and not really caring about the end result, that I finally called it quits. I left that job to pursue an acting career, which was what I had always wanted to do. To support myself and pay the bills, I waited tables and did various odd jobs. Like most actors, I struggled to make any money at it. The jobs I did land paid well, but there were often long dry spells between them. I hung in there because I loved the freedom and sense of aliveness that goes hand in hand with a creative life. Having the opportunity to explore my soul through the literary world of the playwright and then share it with an audience was, at times, a religious experience. The more I trained and grew as an artist, the more I fell in love with the works of Shakespeare and the classical Greeks.

It all changed, though, after performing the role of Cassandra in *The Trojan Women* at the Boston Playwrights Theater. My excitement and passion to share her story through Euripides's esoteric verse didn't go over so well. My loyal friends, who came to all my shows, asked me to never invite them to something like this again. It became clear to me that the painful truths of the spoils of war, such as throwing young children off a cliff, accurately forecasted by a woman deemed crazy, was too much for most to watch. When I could no longer see a future on this career path due to sporadic work, constant rejection, and poor pay, disillusionment struck again.

So like most disillusioned young professionals, I decided to go back to school. Getting a master's degree in clinical mental health counseling helped me to land the most perfect job ever, one that was filled with disillusionment: a methadone clinic. Unlike my previous work venues, there was something both different and special about this latest venture. In the world of sports television, it wasn't safe to speak of the darker truths. In the world of acting, the art and craft itself demands for those truths to be spoken, for without it, there can be no cathartic experience for the audience. In the world of methadone treatment, the darker truths of reality went hand in hand with everyday life for the clients. This acceptance of darker realities followed in suit for the clinicians who worked there and bore witness to their clients' pain.

I spent nine wonderful years there, bearing witness to it all.

When I tell people that I worked at a methadone clinic, they almost always react by saying, "Wow, that must have been rough," which at times it was. They envisioned my clients to be the person they often see nodding off at their local Dunkin Donuts or some man wearing a black ski mask, robbing a drugstore for oxycontin. They then talk of the characters in Ben Affleck's film *The Town*, who were part of the coalition of Charlestown bank robbers, or Martin Scorsese's *The Departed*, which featured members of Whitey Bulger's notorious Winter Hill Gang. Yes, I treated some of those folks, but they were only a small part of my caseload.

What most people don't imagine is the person who is just like you, perhaps a trades worker, teacher, lawyer, professional athlete, or even a medical student who fell on hard times, got sober, and then became actively involved in their professional and family lives. They were the majority of my clients, who all had incredible stories of disillusionment to share and the courage to tell them. When they did so, they would make their clinic colleagues and myself laugh for hours, weep quietly for days, and be struck to the core with horror for a lifetime. Their stories, when shared, had a powerful healing effect on everyone, including me. They offered each other hope.

Through the process of psychotherapy, fostered by a safe clinical environment where everyone was treated respectfully, clients were allowed to be who they were and speak the truth of who they were (good, bad, and ugly), which in turn allowed them to become who they wanted to be. For some, that meant becoming sober. The safe and respectful environment of the agency's outer system trickled down and created a sense of safety for clients to explore the deeper truths of their inner systems.

When I left the clinic to start a private practice, I noticed something profound. The suburbanite clients who now came to see me for their relationship struggles and romantic entanglements, who for the most part were far more socially and economically privileged than those at the methadone clinic, were filled with the worst and quietest sense of desperation that I had ever seen. They felt trapped in their environments, both current and developmental, which didn't foster the safety for them to speak the truth of who they were and who they longed to be. They desperately needed a place, much like the clinic, where they could explore their inner landscapes and understand the darker nature of their longings and desires. Just as my clients at the methadone clinic could tell me about their drug use without moral judgment or repercussion (which in turn helped them get sober), my new clients needed that same safety for their relational woes.

They needed to be able to say things such as "I'm lonely and not sure I want to start over again," or "I don't know if I want to stay married," or "I'm having an affair and I'm not sure I want to stop," or "I think I'm involved with an emotionally abusive and manipulative partner and am not sure what to do" and be met with the same curious and compassionate connection that my methadone clients were. It is this type of connection, one that fosters people's own curiosity about why they feel what they feel and compassion for why they do what they do, that gives them hope. When hope gets discovered, thus begins the inward search for answers to questions that once seemed too dangerous to ask. In time, this translates into a newfound sense of courage, where clients can begin to trust that not only is it okay to be who they want to be and live how they want to live, but it is also an existential necessity.

I once had a mentor at the methadone clinic say to me, "Anonymity isn't always a good thing." I believe this to be true. Our stories matter, including the choices we make that create them and the courage we have to share them, whether they are dark and tragic, fun and inspiring, or even seemingly humdrum and ordinary. When written, spoken, and shared, they have power. This power allows some to heal and inspires others to do the same. It can create a sense of empathy and connection toward those who come from different backgrounds and have different ideas about what it means to be alive and how we should act, particularly in our personal and romantic relationships. It helps give us the courage to ask the most important existential question of all, one that only we can answer ourselves: "What must I do?"

When my friend told me that I was closer than I thought to finishing my book, she helped me see that the book was already written in my blog and that I needed to find a way to thread those stories into a cohesive book. This made my heart lift. Excitement and inspiration began to move through me again as I found the hope in my professional crisis. So that is what I did.

I share the story of my personal journey in my professional background because some of the blog posts use sports metaphors; others examine themes in films, internet folklore, and even slices of life from the methadone world. Many start with song lyrics because, as Friedrich Nietzsche said, "A life without music would be a mistake."

As a woman who worked in sports television when it was considered unconventional, performed in Greek drama, and worked in a methadone clinic, disillusionment has served me well. It has given me an affinity for going against the grain, which allows me to help others do the same, should that be something they really want and need to do. I say this not to cause trouble (that's the last thing that I want), but because I think people get into trouble when they live other people's realities and not their own. I experienced this personally when I stayed in a job in sports television long after I knew I no longer wanted to remain in that field. For me, disillusionment over time turned into inspiration. I learned that through disillusionment, a necessary breakdown of a false self takes place, which always gives way to a true one, whether it be on an individual, cultural, or global level. I believe it's an important rite of passage for people to experience, which is why I share it. There's such a raw honesty to it, which I think the world desperately needs these days.

When people have the courage to journey through this rite of passage and share it with others, I believe it grants a necessary implicit permission to others, including perhaps you, to do the same. This journey involves discovering new possibilities and ways of being in this world that you didn't know were available to you. Knowing that it is can give you the tiny bit of courage you may need to disavow a quiet life of desperation and take a chance on living the authentic life your soul craves. Authenticity, while not easy, can become contagious. And I think that's a good thing.

All it takes is hope and courage.

INTRODUCTION

In the middle of a crisis lies an opportunity.
—Albert Einstein

I am a hope merchant.[i]

I have written a book that intends to sell you hope. My sales strategy, which will help you decide whether or not you really want to buy it, is to tell you stories of hope: hope that's lost, hope that's found, and most importantly, the story of hope itself. My job as a hope merchant, which I perform under the nom de plume of psychotherapist, is to help people find hope when they need it most. It's why they come to see me in the first place. I must confess something first, though, a caveat before you read on. What I honestly sell and what people honestly invest in, week after week and year after year, boils down to something simple. It's the oldest sales tactic in the world: a bait and switch. Please allow me the privilege to explain to you, as I make a pitch for hope in the next hundred-and-something pages, what exactly that switch is.

Most people come to therapy when they are in a crisis. In my practice, more often than not, it's a crisis involving the pain of lost love. In keeping with the theme of storytelling, I will refer to these crises in different chapters of this book as the story of love's labor's lost. Desperately seeking some way to make sense of their situation, which often presents itself in the agonizing packages of human loneliness, infidelity, divorce, or dealing with a manipulative partner, they tell me their stories, and I listen. I listen, with an ear tuned into to the sounds of their inner orchestra and the song it longs to write, sing, and play. From a psychodynamic perspective, I listen to how developed that orchestra is and what notes it gets stuck on. From an Internal Family Systems perspective, I listen to the sounds different members of that inner orchestra make, what instruments they play, and how connected they are to their creative source. From an existential perspective, I listen to the pain and longing they have to write, play, and sing that one song they feel destined to do so, before time runs out. From a somatic perspective, I listen to the hidden notes locked in the tension and sensations in their bodies. From a feminist perspective, I listen to the notes of inequality, oppression, and social injustice that want a measure or two in that song. And last but not least, from an ecological systems perspective, I listen to the sounds of the outer systems that influence each client's inner jam band, including their family, community, and culture at large.

Through this long and often arduous process of systemic listening, fearless exploring, and welcomed discovering, my clients find enough compassion and hope to hear the music too. Then they understand the story behind the story of their inner song and realize how that song drove them to the crossroads where they now find themselves. Through their connection to hope and compassion, creative solutions to their polarized problems begin to appear, and the authentic choices they long to make becomes less daunting. With hope, accompanied by compassion, they then find the courage to choose for themselves which road to take, which direction best leads them out of their crises, and what songs to put on their play list as they prepare to ride on.

When I applied to graduate school for clinical psychology in 2002, I had to answer the following question: what theories about psychology do you believe help people to change? I answered, I believe most people don't want to change. What they want is to be who they really are and live the life they most want to live. Therapy, in my view, helps dissipate the fear that keeps people from being and doing just that.

Sixteen years later, I still believe what I wrote then. When clients come to therapy to "free themselves, so they can be themselves,"[ii] in a hermeneutic sense, they do change, by becoming who they really are.

I can't think of a better way to start this book off than with a story about a forgotten song of lost courage and dashed hope. Obviously, it's not a fun or happy story. On the contrary, it's a devastating tale on which modern psychotherapy was founded. It exemplifies the longitudinal legacy of devastating consequences that can take place when one chooses inauthentically. It's a story about a crisis experienced by none other than Sigmund Freud.

Most know of Freud as the founder of psychoanalysis, the therapeutic methodology devised to uproot inner conflict which has influenced many modern psychotherapies. Some know about his theories on unconscious sexual drives and the Oedipal complex. Some know that he narrowly escaped the Nazi invasion of Europe and spent his short-lived remaining time in England, where he succumbed to throat cancer and died through assisted suicide.

Very few, however, know the story about a fatalistic choice he once had to make.

Sigmund Freud's Choice

Judith Herman, author of *Trauma and Recovery: The Aftermath of Violence*,[iii] dedicates the first chapter in her book to Freud's choice. Poignantly called "A Forgotten History," Herman details a trip Freud made in the late 1800s to an asylum in France called Salpetriere. It was under the medical directorship of Jean-Martin Charcot. During the last two decades of the nineteenth century in Europe, there was epidemic of hysteria among women, many of whom were sent to this asylum. Freud, who sought to understand the root cause of this hysteria, chose to spend time there, as did many other physicians at the time, including Pierre Janet and William James.

Freud was born, raised, and educated in Vienna, Austria; at that time, he was a rising star in the field of neurology. Janet was a notable physician, as well. They both discovered something profound and developed the same hypothesis, when treating these women.

What they discovered was, these women were trauma survivors. They suffered through horrific violence including rape, incest, and other kinds of abuse. Too terrified to speak of their experiences, which would result in more abuse, they stayed quiet. With little options for them, they continued living with their abusers, who for the most part were men. This, in turn, perpetuated their cycles of abuse. Because their hysteria made it difficult for these women to remain living in their homes, they were sent away to Salpetriere. Freud, who was becoming a master of understanding unconscious expressions of pain, cracked the coded language of their hysterical symptoms. He discovered that their unexpressed psychic pain became physical pain and concluded the hysteria was a somatic expression of it. These women were showing, rather than telling, the tale of what happened to them. The hysteria also created a secondary gain for these women, as the asylum was a much better living option for them. It kept them away from their abusers.

In the well-documented case of Anna O., whom Freud collaborated on with Joseph Breuer, this patient began to heal, through various therapeutic techniques. In 1896, Freud published *The Aetiology of Hysteria,* case studies from his time spent at Salpetriere, in which he concluded his findings of the connection between hysteria and abuse.

A year later, he recanted his theory.

There has been much speculation for his reason to do this, as he wasn't one to kowtow to any kind of systemic disapproval. Yet he may have in this regard, as some have argued. All we really know is that he did, but we don't have the full and complete picture on why. Here, however, is one highly plausible explanation:

Concerned about the implications of his discovery, Freud found himself in a pickle. Should he stick to what he knew to be true, which would not go over well in patriarchal Europe, or change his mind and not disrupt the cultural norms in order to have a notable career? Not knowing how to deal with such a heavy burden, as the consequences for following his intuition could have ended his career and ruined his reputation, he chose the latter. He changed his theory and concluded the women he treated imagined their abuse.

Some believe the only way Freud could continue to live in a patriarchal society, given what he knew, was to turn a blind eye to it. Echoing Sophocles's King Oedipus, who blinded himself after he learned the truth of what he had done, fulfilling the oracle's prophecy of killing his father and marrying his mother, Freud metaphorically blinded himself as well. The truth of what he had witnessed and learned may have been just too horrific and threatening to continue looking at.

Once the champion of these women, he became their betrayer when he rejected his own hypothesis. Instead of killing his father to marry is mother, in Oedipal fashion, he killed the feminine in order to remain loyal to the masculine: the patriarchal culture. One could argue the aftermath of his choice was both tragic and profound.

A few years later, after Freud had achieved high-ranking status as a psychiatrist and his psychoanalytic methodology became the treatment modality for neurosis, another up-and-coming physician found himself in a career-changing double bind, as well. His name was Carl Jung, and he was Freud's protégé.

What has been described as an intense professional love affair between these two men, where Jung claimed he had a "religious crush"[iv] on Freud, eventually ended in contention. While much has been written about Jung possibly being anti-Semitic, a philanderer, and not any kind of advocate for women suffering from hysteria, he did develop ideas of his own that deviated from Freud's unconscious theory of sexual drives. Some of these ideas included synchronicity, archetypes, and his belief in the collective unconscious, which he most likely formulated by studying world mythology. The collective unconscious basically alleges that we channel ancestral memories and act them out in our lives. This renegade idea did not go over well at all with Freud, whose life's work was founded on his theory of the personal unconscious, which he believed people acted out. Philosophically speaking, Freud was an atheist, and Jung was not, which made it hard for Freud to tolerate Jung's metaphysical views. At a crossroad, Jung had a choice to make: deny what his heart and mind believed to be right (just as Freud did) and have a comfortable life as psychoanalyst, or risk Freud's disapproval and his career, to stay true to what he wanted. What did he do? He found the hope he needed to follow his heart and the courage to do just that.

Though ostracized by his mentor and the psychoanalytic community, in the long run, Jung did just fine. He developed his own style of psychotherapy, called Jungian analysis, which explores the mythological archetypes of the collective unconscious that he had a passionate faith in. Though it's not a widely practiced form of treatment these days (nor is traditional psychoanalysis, for that matter), Jung's ideas have had great influence on the transpersonal psychology movement, where spirituality and psychology meet.

Did Freud make the right choice? It's easy to say no, he didn't. Going against the grain and not caving to the pressures that societal and cultural norms exert always poses a threat to one's social identity and survival. It was terrifying then, and it's terrifying now. While the cultural tide of resistance and speaking truth to power is changing in the United States, with the #Me Too and #Times Up movements, when it comes to matters of the heart, many people still sell out by doing what others want them to do, like staying in a relationship when they want to leave or leaving one when they want to stay. Choices matter, and they do have a reverberating effect.

What if Freud had the courage to stand by what he discovered? What if he remained the champion of these women, rather than their betrayer? Given the considerable influence his ideas have had over the past hundred and more years, it's fair to say his blaming of the victim has had just as much of an impact. For years, women and men have remained silent about their abuse, in fear that they wouldn't be believed or would even be blamed for it. Had Freud made a different choice, would sexual abuse, human trafficking, and other violent sex crimes exist on the grand scale they do today? Would the Catholic church sex abuse scandal have grown to the epic proportion that it did? Could the forty-year Penn State sex abuse scandal have been prevented? Would two powerful men, both accused of rape and serial sexual assault, have been able to become the president of the United States of America?

We will never know.

We can, however, learn from it and commit to an idea that Albert Einstein once shared, as he knew that all problems had "creative solutions." He knew, however, that solutions to one's problems could not be discovered with the same consciousness that created them in the first place. Freud failed to find his solution, but you can succeed in finding yours.

What This Book Offers

I believe when people find themselves in a crisis of love's labor's lost, they have an opportunity to do something grand for themselves. If this happens to be you, this book will show you how to find the hope to do just that. Once you find it, you can then discover creative solutions to seemingly impossible problems. Psychotherapy, when done well, facilitates that search. With the right therapist and an honest will, looking inside oneself can soothe the stress response to the crises that made everything seem hopeless and impossible in the first place. This in turn allows for open and curious inner state of being—hope, per se—and then that's when the good stuff happens.

This book offers examples and stories of how that search took place for many of my clients and how they found hope in their crisis. By engaging and staying in the process of therapy, they were able to do the inner work they needed to do. Once they found hope, they also discovered the "creative solutions" they needed. This helped them make authentic choices and live the lives they wanted to live rather than what others wanted for them. The blog posts in each chapter, which the book itself grew out of, will be called the "Feature Story," in keeping with a mock sports broadcast style. Many chapters will also have some color commentary to highlight particular points. These featured stories express both my creative process and my experience with some tough cases, where I found myself joining with my clients' pain as they grappled to make meaning of it. Each post is prefaced with the story behind the story, combined with clinical theory and practice to help readers better understand how the process of psychotherapy works. The facts of all the cases presented here have been changed to protect the identity and confidentiality of my clients. Since I often work clinically with metaphor, many of these pieces do, as well.

"Part 1: The Crisis: When Love's Labor's Lost" begins with one of the oldest and most influential stories of love, loss, crisis, and hope: the myth of Cupid and Psyche. Moving systemically from the outside in, the relentless pursuit for hope will be viewed through both feminist and ecological lenses, highlighting the ancestral legacy of this story and its long-term effect. It then shifts gears to teach, from traditional psychodynamic and phenomenological lenses, a different pathway to hope. It explains how one's relationship map gets created in childhood and then activated in adulthood, with case examples. It shows how these maps have compasses embedded in them that lead people down the pathway to the many crises of love's labor's loss, including having a manipulative or abusive partner, infidelity, divorce, or being alone and starting over.

"Part 2: Hope" tells the original story of hope, found in the myth of Pandora. It begins to integrate the therapeutic models described in part 1 with the Internal Family Systems (IFS) model of psychotherapy, founded by Richard Schwartz. Here, clients delve deeper into the process of self-discovery in psychotherapy, where the recalibration of one's internal compass and relationship map begins to take place. It gives clinical examples of clients working somatically, illustrating what happens when they discover an inner resource inside of them, one that becomes a game changer.

"Part 3: Courage" begins with the Hindu myth of Ganesha, the elephant god who removes obstacles. He epitomizes courage. Here, hope teams up with courage to help people discover the real road to love's labor's won, by authentically recalibrating their internal compass and relationship maps. It shares case study examples of this and the creative solutions that arose from it.

So there you have it: an introductory sales pitch and an invitation to learn more. I know that many people say, "Hope is not a strategy," but I intend to prove otherwise. Should you find yourself stuck in a crisis involving love's labor's lost, and you hope to get back on your feet so you can play in the game again, this book can help. Hope is always there, inside of you, and when you find it, you will find a winning solution too.

Are you ready?

If so, stand by to go live in four, three, two, one...

PART 1

The Crisis: When Love's Labor Is Lost

CHAPTER 1

Mythology and Modern Love

An Ancient Perspective on Why the Course of True Love Doesn't Always Run Smooth

Now that you've been introduced to the seldom-told story of Freud (and if you have no idea what I am talking about, please go back and read the introduction), you may have a sense of how his choice to turn a blind eye to what he discovered played a role in the continued legacy of sexual abuse against both women and men. By reinforcing the learned behavior of silence when one experiences or witnesses trauma, I believe this silencing has trickled down into individuals and family systems, where many people in relationships either deny their thoughts, feelings, and behaviors or just don't know how to talk about them. Modern psychotherapy in the West was founded on this denial of facts. Trauma (more on this in chapter 2), more specifically, trauma in one's early attachment, writes the scripts that people act from when they find themselves traveling down the road of love's labor's lost.

There are more contributing plots in this script, though, which feminists have been saying for years. Now, it's not my intention to shame anyone about anything, only to open people's eyes a little wider to these perspectives which, until recently, have been consistently dismissed. Two story lines that get overlooked in the modern-day crises of love's labor's lost, including starting over, manipulative or abusive partners, infidelity, and divorce, are the ancestral legacies of patriarchy, which grants more power and privilege to men, and misogyny, particularly the denial of it, where women are seen as objects of pleasure rather than equal contributing partners.

Many of the stories I share in this book will speak for themselves in this regard. Again, I will offer some chapter color commentary to highlight these factors and help emphasize some of the nuanced and not-so-nuanced ways in which women are still truly disadvantaged.

In graduate school, we were taught that from an ecological cultural perspective, all the systems in the world influencing our lives are constantly interacting with each other. These systems include global, national, regional, educational, family, and one's inner system. Shifts and changes in one of the spheres of the system inevitably contribute to shifts and changes in the others. Psychotherapy, for the most part, deals with the inner system of clients, their partners, and their families. It's what I work with in my practice.

Addressing the outer system, though, is not something I can really do with clients who have variant social or political views. It's my job to be both curious and respectful of those views. Still, I see it as part of the problem and an important piece of the puzzle in the crises of love's labor's lost. My creative solution, therefore, in addressing it, is to start and end this book by sharing, from feminist and ecological perspectives, one of the oldest stories about love relationships that is known in the West. It's a story that Freud was well versed in too: Apuleius's *Cupid and Psyche*.

Cupid and Psyche

In this myth,[v,vi] Cupid quietly defies his mother, Venus, who is the goddess of love and attraction. Jealous of Psyche's beauty, which many mortals claim rivals her own, Venus orders Cupid to humiliate Psyche by making her fall madly in love with a beast. When he tries to carry out the order, he accidentally pricks himself on his own arrow and falls in love with Psyche. Not ready to deal with the wrath of his mother should she learn of his betrayal or the public's perception of such, he marries Psyche in secret but requires her to never look upon his face. She agrees to this at

first but then has second thoughts after listening to her sisters' concerns that she may have married a monster. She wants to know and see who she is married to.

One night, while Cupid is sleeping, Psyche chooses to openly defy Cupid's request of her and lights a lantern to spy upon his face. She instantly falls in love with him. This love is short-lived, however, as a drop of oil from the lantern falls on Cupid and burns him, waking him from his sleep. Angry at Psyche's betrayal, he abandons her.

Psyche, pregnant with Cupid's child and desperate to get him back, first prays to Ceres, the goddess of motherly relationships, and then Juno, the goddess of marriage, asking for their help. While they are both sympathetic to Psyche's cause, they refuse to defy Venus. This forces Psyche to go to Venus herself. When Venus learns the truth of what happened, that her son betrayed her and married her mortal rival, she flies into a jealous rage. She beats Psyche, with the help of her handmaidens, Anxiety and Melancholy. After torturing Psyche, Venus agrees to help her if she can complete the following task: sort an enormous pile of grains before sundown, a task that ten people could not possibly complete.

Yet an ant takes pity on Psyche and recruits its colony to do the work. When Venus returns home to see that Psyche has successfully completed the assignment, she gives her another impossible task. She tells Psyche to cross a river to a field where some rare but dangerous sheep graze and to bring her back some of their golden fleece. Knowing this would kill her, Psyche attempts to kill herself by throwing herself into the river. The river reeds, however, take pity on her and come to life. They tell her how she can get the fleece without harming herself.

When Psyche returns to Venus with the fleece, she gets assigned an even more dangerous job: to fill a flask of water from the River Styx by climbing over a dangerous mountain range filled with wild beasts and dragons. Psyche begins to climb the mountain and soon realizes she will fall to her death. Jupiter then takes pity on Psyche and sends his eagle to get the water for her. When Psyche returns, Venus, who is dumbfounded by her continued success, gives her one final and fatal task.

She demands that Psyche journey to the underworld, where no mortal has ever returned from, in order to get Cupid back. The objective of this journey was to bring Venus back a sample of beauty from the underworld's

Queen Proserpina. Once again, Psyche believes she will die trying, so she climbs a tower and prepares again to take her own life. This time, the tower takes pity on her and comes to life. The tower tells her the secret to getting in and out of the underworld and how to retrieve the sample of beauty. He warns her, though, not to open the sample of beauty. Psyche agrees. After conquering all the hurdles on her journey to the underworld, she succeeds in retrieving the sample. Curious about how the sample might help her win back the love of Cupid, she defies the tower's order and opens it. What's inside sends her into a deep sleep.

When Cupid finally heals from his burn, he realizes how much he misses Psyche. He searches for her and finds her asleep, near death. He pricks her with his arrow and wakes her up. Returning her from the underworld, he then tries to get consent from the gods to make his marriage legitimate. Jupiter, who is married to Juno, makes a deal with Cupid. He will agree to let him marry Psyche, provided Cupid assist him with capturing the hearts of other women (without Juno's knowledge, of course) so that he could have dalliances at his will. Cupid agrees to Jupiter's terms, and with the help of the god Mercury, they get Venus to back off for good.

Well, there's much to say here. Traditionally, this story has been used to teach of the many stages of love relationships, including attraction, infatuation, commitment, betrayal, rejection, loss, rediscovery, redemption, forgiveness, and reunion. Cupid and Psyche find each other, lose each other, courageously bear the pain of the loss of each other, and then find each other once again. They prove they can reinvent their relationship—which couples need to do for their love to last because as people grow and change over time, so do their wants, needs, and desires. Their reinvention arises after time, space, and a journey to the underworld, which, in modern days, would be psychotherapy.

This story also captures the underpinnings of the crises in modern relationships. It illustrates the challenges Psyche has when Cupid leaves her. It details how hard it was for her to start over. It shows Venus's abuse and manipulation of Psyche as well as Jupiter's unabashed willingness to cheat on his wife.

Alternatively, this story emphasizes both the importance and the challenge of what Shakespeare's Polonius advised to his son Laertes: "To thine own self be true." Cupid and Psyche find their happiness together when they do just that and ignore what others want for them.

And yes, the myth also speaks to the gender inequality between women and men. Psyche is tormented, abused, and almost put to death because another woman, Venus, is overcome by rage and jealousy. She's rescued by a man, Cupid, who falls in love with her and marries her. She becomes subjugated to him when she agrees to the inequitable terms of the marriage, which forbid her from seeing what he looks like. She's then punished not once, but twice when she acts on her curiosity, first to see her husband's face and then later when she opens the box of beauty from Queen Proserpina—an act of defiance that nearly kills her.

She also tries to kill herself several times after Cupid abandons her, in part because of Venus's abuse. We could also argue, though, that her identity is so anchored in that relationship and she doesn't have an individuated sense of self, which would allow her to move on and live her life without him. So she puts herself through Olympian hell-hoops to try to get Cupid back. Sound familiar?

Cupid, on the other hand, has it much easier. His physical pain to heal is a burn wound. Emotionally, he has to mend his broken heart. One could argue he's a bit of a coward, which comes with immaturity. Afraid of the consequences should he openly defy his mother, he marries Psyche secretly. He takes total control of the relationship by making Psyche promise not to look upon his face. Constantly fearing his mother's wrath, he doesn't allow his wife to see him and get to know him in any meaningful way. He also has no empathy for her or room for forgiving her when she breaks her promise and acts, choosing to be true to herself. Cupid does grieve Psyche's loss and misses her when she's gone, a process that makes him decide to get her back. But that's the extent of his suffering, which pales in comparison to hers. And in spite of everything she goes through to get him back, he gets to rescue her once again and be her hero. Isn't that ironic?

He does transform through his grief, though. He figures out a way to make their relationship legitimate and more equitable, and Psyche becomes immortal. He wouldn't have been able to make this happen, however, if he didn't make a deal with Jupiter and agree to help the king of the gods engage in marital indiscretions.

5

Now, for those who find themselves thinking, *It's just a story—and not really relevant to modern love*, then let me present some other ancient facts that have also trickled down into today to strengthen the case.

The customs and mythologies of ancient Greece and Rome have influenced modern Western society, in more ways than love and marriage. Greece and Rome had the earliest democracies, Greece with the Athenian democracy and Rome with its republic. Though both societies were polytheistic, with a pantheon of gods and goddesses to worship and great stories about them to help explain the mysteries of the universe and human behavior, their mythology was patriarchal and hierarchical. With the male gods Zeus and Jupiter bequeathed with the most power and the female goddesses with less, their mythological patriarchies seemed to make their ways into daily life, as women could not participate in their democratic governments. They weren't even allowed to vote. This was true in the United States for a long time.

According to Carol Gilligan, feminist psychologist and co-author of *The Deepening Darkness: Patriarchy, Resistance, and Democracy's Future*,[vii] the ancient customs of Greece and Rome also influenced Freud, as most notably evidenced by his ideas on the Oedipal complex, taken from Sophocles's *Oedipus Rex*. Gilligan also argues something very important in her book, one that speaks to misogyny that women have for each other. She states Aeschylus's trilogy *The Orestia* is haunted with a "history of trauma and separation of both men and women from women." This is evident in the way Venus treats Psyche. Many antagonistic mother-daughter relationships, where the mothers (or stepmothers or mothers-in-law) treat their daughters cruelly, have been born out of this myth. *Cinderella* and *Snow White and the Seven Dwarfs* are two. This type of hateful mother-daughter legacy, which has been passed down over the centuries, will be discussed more in the next chapter.

Finishing up on the tale of Cupid and Psyche, it's important to note that the two lovers triumph when (and only when) they defy what others want of them and do what's right for themselves. Many might argue that the heavy emotional price wasn't worth it.

With that in consideration, one must then ask, what are the consequences for those who choose to conform and not be true to their hearts? Is it nobler to suffer?

Edith Wharton's Pulitzer Prize-winning novel *The Age of Innocence* answers that question. Here she tells the story of Newland Archer, who's engaged to marry May Welland and secure his social position as part of New York's upper-class elite. While engaged, he falls in love with May's cousin, Ellen Olenska, who defied the patriarchal rules of marriage by leaving her abusive husband. She sought Newland's legal help to obtain her freedom by getting divorced. When asked if he believed women should be granted the same freedoms as men (in their affairs), Newland acknowledges that he does. Caving to the family pressure to avoid a scandal, he goes against what he believes is right and advises Ellen not to seek a divorce. He tells her, "Though the laws support divorce, the social customs don't."[viii] Ellen acquiesced and followed Newland's advice. She knew that leaving her husband put a scandalous spotlight on her family, and she did not want to cause them any more shame. This, however, made it impossible for Ellen to ever marry again. If she wanted love from a partner, she could be a mistress but not a wife.

Newland does marry May, but in time, he realizes it was a mistake. His heart and soul are with Ellen. Not wanting to live a life with him as his mistress, she agrees to consummate their love only once and then leave forever, but their plans get thwarted. Desperate to be with her, Newland does try to leave May. Yet the family, who has suspected an affair between the two, makes it next to impossible for them. They do what it takes to force Newland to stay with May, honoring the unwritten rule "Better a life without love than love without honor."[ix] Newland succumbs to his fate, makes his life all about his kids; he lives a life of quiet desperation. It's an existential tragedy.

If you had to choose between being true to yourself and defying the rules, as Cupid and Psyche did, or conforming to them, believing it's somehow nobler to suffer, as Newland did, neither seems ideal. It's a common polarization in the modern crisis of love's labor's lost. Yet Gilligan also notes that defiance, by women and men, even in ancient times, has always been part of the solution. Throughout time, writers, painters, actors, and musicians have been creatively defying and addressing social issues, including the crises of love and its loss, through their artwork. It's their collective creative solution, intended to give us all hope, which, in turn, sparks change.

Color Commentary

This play has worked. The steadfast creative defiance of artists throughout the years, coupled with the unwavering defiance of social activists, has created more collective hope today than ever before. The world continues to change before our very own eyes, as evidenced by the #metoo and #times up movements. It's changing from an ecological systemic perspective, and misogyny is finally starting to get taken seriously. Will this change trickle down to the inner systems of relational dynamics? Yes, but the crises of love's labor's lost are multilayered, and the systemic addressing of misogyny on a macro level is only one part in finding the creative solution.

With that said, let's now explore the makings of our relational inner systems: our relationship maps with embedded internal compasses that direct us toward particular people and particular circumstances. It's an important layer that therapists get to exclusively address. The next chapter details how these maps get created and how they contribute to crises of love's labor's lost. Though what's about to come next does amplify the steepness of the challenges that contribute to the problem, don't worry. Hope is on the way.

CHAPTER 2

Alone Again and Starting Over: Lessons on Love and Attachment

All, everything I understand, I only understand because I love.
—Leo Tolstoy

"I'm too young to be a widower and too old to have my heartbroken like a teenager," Ted said softly, as he held back tears while sitting on my couch. At age fifty-eight and fresh off an unsuccessful stint of internet dating, which he tried two years after his wife died, Ted came to see me in despair. He had been married twice, as he and his first wife divorced; he had started a new relationship with someone he met online that didn't work out.

Jenny came to see me when she found herself in the same crisis as Ted. She had left her abusive husband for her lover, who then turned out to be a covert version of her husband. He then left her for someone else. At age forty-three, after having two significant relationships that left her deeply wounded, Jenny tried online dating and soon got scared off by some of the lewd messages she found in her inbox. Struggling with the thought of starting over yet again, Jenny and Ted both struggled with the idea of possibly spending the rest of their lives alone.

"Can things actually work out after opening day?" Ted asked me.

"Will I ever meet my soulmate online and at my age?" Jenny wondered out loud.

These two clients, both of whom were baseball fanatics and loved talking sports in session, found themselves in a common crisis of love's labor's lost: Starting over.

Like many people, Ted and Jenny didn't really understand the different stages in a relationship, what people act out with each other during their season together, why they do that, and how to learn from the errors they make. They both wondered if they would ever have a winning season.

The anecdotal view that I get from my chair with clients experiencing this kind of crisis has become more and more common, with divorce rates ever climbing. The cacophony of sorrow from this crisis often sounds like a song out of tune and off the beat, with people chronically stuck on the same painful note. Coupled with the illusion of more and seemingly better options always available by swiping right on a dating app, the cadence of "now, now, now" and "more, more, more" is not in sync with the rhythms of the human heart. Online dating, which has many benefits, including accessibility to meeting more people, also has some drawbacks. It creates the illusion that there's always something better out there. Today's technology doesn't teach how to nurture and develop deep, intimate connections with the perfectly imperfect person you may be starting over with. Psychotherapy, however, does.

New relationships can feel both exciting and daunting for anyone at any time in the lifespan. If you've experienced a lot of heartache in the past or have had a history of complicated relationships, starting over may feel worse than pulling teeth. The key to managing this crisis without it feeling so dreadful is to understand your attachment style and the relational patterns you act out as a result of it. So what exactly is that?

Attachment Theory Made Simple

Simply put, how you were loved by your parents or caretakers in childhood is how you love. You are drawn to what you know on a primal level. It's part of your relationship map, embedded with an internal compass that directs you toward people whose internal compasses and maps feel similar to yours. Let me explain.

From infancy through early childhood, the quality of connection children have with their primary caretakers shapes and forms their senses of self. If their needs are met (when they cry, they are held and soothed; when hungry, fed; and when alert, played and communicated with), they begin to develop a sense of safety and trust in their immediate world around them, which is merged with that of their primary caretaker. As an infant, this connection is first experienced through touch. How a parental figure holds them gets soaked up like sponge as they absorb the love (or lack thereof), anxiety (or calmness), detachment (or attachment), and all the other complicated feelings that parents and caretakers have toward their children that are both explicitly and implicitly expressed during their formative years.

While much has been written about this post-Freud period from many notable psychologists, including Melanie Klein and Margaret Mahler, whose work will be discussed in the next chapters, here are some basic ideas on attachment and childhood development from two British psychoanalysts: Donald Winnicott and John Bowlby. While they had different thoughts on the subject, their work has greatly influenced modern psychotherapy.

The Influences of Donald Winnicott and John Bowlby

Both of these men understood that ruptures in the infant's and child's attachments to their parental figures affects them throughout the lifespan, particularly their capacity for love and intimacy as adults.

Now, no one has had perfect parenting. There is no such thing. And this is not about parent bashing. It's about examining one's first experience of love, attachment, and connection that gets reenacted in adult relationships. Plus, all anyone needs is "good enough" parenting, which many get, but some don't. Good enough parenting is a saying that therapists use to describe how attuned and attentive a child's caretakers were: not overly stimulating or neglectful and capable of showing love and setting behavioral limits. Now before jumping into theory and science, here's a visual that might help:

Imagine a mother or father holding a newborn, gazing down upon their precious little face. They are head over heels in love with their child and are reasonably unstressed in their day-to-day lives. What do you imagine that newborn takes in and learns about itself? It learns how lovable it is. Now imagine that same newborn with an overly anxious parent, perhaps due to financial stress or a problematic relationship with the other parent, who nonetheless still loves and welcomes their child.

What do you now imagine that child takes in? It might take in that it is lovable, but not all the time. Next, picture a mother with postpartum depression or a depressed parent, who also loves their child. Imagine that parent holding their little one with their depressed gaze? What might that newborn experience? It might experience that it is not lovable or is the cause of is caretaker's unhappiness.

You can apply this same visual with all kinds of parenting scenarios, including a parent with a trauma or addiction history that's now gotten triggered by this birth, or even a parent who didn't want a child in the first place and neglects it. Now imagine the same quality of connection through the various parenting styles when a child develops. What kinds of beliefs might a child develop that aren't true but seem so at the time?

English pediatrician and psychoanalyst Donald Winnicott, whose signature ideas on holding, good enough parenting, and how a true self develops through creative play and possibility in childhood, has written much about this. He hypothesized[x,xi] "how safe and secure" children could feel in their bodies and minds depended upon how they were held, both physically and emotionally, as they developed. If parents had consistent (not perfect) attunement with their child's physical and emotional needs, gave them attentive space to play and explore their world without being overly protective, set loving limits, and allowed the child to be whoever it wanted, the child would develop a true self. With a true self, that child would feel a sense of aliveness that fostered spontaneous expressions of feelings and creativity. If this parenting style remains consistent (again, not perfect), as children grow into perfectly imperfect adults, they will feel safe enough to do this in adult relationships, as that was their relational model and experience of love. They will develop a secure attachment style and have an innate skill that allows for strong intimate bonds and authentic relating, which tends to fare well in marriage and long-term partnerships. It's been encoded in their internal relationship compass and map.

Winnicott believed the reverse to be also true, asserting complications in the parent-child attachment through inconsistent holding (think of the above visual for this); misattunements; and lack of attention, communication, and play fostered a sense of anxiety and lack of safety in the child's body and mind. As children grow and organize around the parent's complex style, they often develop what Winnicott calls a "false self," where they learn to express feelings that comply with the parent's expectations, implicitly knowing their own feelings might not be accepted. As adults, these relational patterns resulting from an insecure attachment style pose obstacles to authentic intimate connection, as they too will comply with others' expectations and put their own feelings aside. Here, many problems are born that hinder adult intimacy, including codependency, addiction, and serial infidelity, as they too are part of their internal compass and relationship map.

John Bowlby, another psychoanalyst, became interested in human relational cartography when he developed attachment theory. After his psychoanalytical training, Bowlby studied ethnology (animal behavior) as well as evolutionary biology and Darwinism. He observed how newborn goslings attached to their mothers, which had to happen during a certain time frame or they wouldn't attach at all. Attached goslings would follow their mothers, and unattached ones wouldn't. He then applied this to parent-child attachment. In keeping with Winnicott's ideas on good enough parenting and holding environments, Bowlby examined the level of anxiety and stress children experienced when separated for extended periods of time from their parents and how they expressed that anxiety. He experimented in learning from an evolutionary biological perspective how secure attachment developed in humans.

His work got further developed by psychologist Mary Ainsworth, who conducted a famous (in the psychotherapy world, that is) longitudinal study called the Strange Situation.

The Strange Situation

This study, initially conducted in Baltimore in the 1950s, has been repeated hundreds of times by developmental psychologists throughout the world, with similar findings. Ainsworth, who was studying the mother-infant attachment in the first year of life, developed a twenty-minute scenario for the mother and child to participate with. Candidates were selected after one year of in-home observations of the mother-infant relationship. During the actual procedure, the mother and infant would enter the laboratory, where there would be toys for the infant to play with. A stranger would then be introduced to the scene while the child was playing. Then, the mother would leave the room for up to three minutes and then return. The level of distress the child would feel when left and upon reunion fell into distinct distress behavior patterns. Ainsworth concluded the following:[xii]

1. Children with a *secure inner attachment* (good enough parenting or holding environment) would show signs of missing the mother during the separation and cry. When the mother returned, they initiated contact with her and, once soothed, went back to playing with toys.

2. Children with an *insecure avoidant attachment* (not good enough parenting or holding environment) would show little distress upon separation and ignored the mother when she returned.

3. Children with an *insecure anxious ambivalent attachment* (not good enough parenting or holding environment) would be worried prior to the separation and did not explore or play much with toys available for them, as they were hyper focused on their mothers. They seemed angry or preoccupied when the mother left and had difficulty being soothed upon reunion, showing little interest in returning to explore the environment or play with the toys.

4. Children with an ***insecure disorganized attachment*** (results from an abusive environment), which was discovered later, displayed myriad behaviors, including disorienting and dissociative (trance state) behaviors, combined sometimes with excessive clinging or crying. They may move toward the parent but look in the opposite direction, displaying a push-pull message of "come here, go away." This pattern leans toward a probability of child abuse.

The Science behind Relationship Maps

Psychiatrist Daniel Siegel delves into the neuroscience behind attachment styles (relationship maps) in his book *The Developing Mind*.[xiii] Here, he makes the case that the quality and style of attachment that children develop become part of their implicit memory (unconscious memory), as do the ruptures in that attachment. While not conscious, these implicit memories cannot be expressed verbally, but rather they are somatically felt through discomfort, tension, and other sensations in the body.

When people complain to me of their aches and pains that their doctors can't get to the bottom of, I start to wonder what's going on at home with their partner. When I ask, they say things such as, "I don't know. I have a good marriage; I don't know why I'm unhappy." Then the stories they tell me suggest quite the opposite. Their bodies absorb the unhappiness that they are not yet ready to feel.

Adults with insecure attachment styles tend to be attracted to partners who trigger those implicit memories. The due north on their individual compasses embedded in their relationship maps becomes calibrated toward each other, often led by intense chemistry. This chemistry can make it difficult to leave, even when their rational mind knows they should. Ever have a friend who ends up in the same type of bad relationship over and over again, which makes you scratch your head with confusion? Freud understood why people often get stuck on the same sour note over and over again in their relationships, and he developed a theory for it.

The Repetition Compulsion

When people feel like it's Groundhog Day all over again with their partners, acting out the same fight or being drawn to the same kind of person who really isn't good for them, then they are indeed stuck in a repetitive pattern, which therapists call the repetition compulsion.

Freud concluded that people repeat in the present what they can't remember from their past, in an insanely impossible effort to master something traumatic that already happened so therefore can't be mastered, which is why it is a compulsion.[xiv] He understood that this trauma became a part of someone's relationship map, though he didn't use that verbiage. He also believed the driving force of the repetition compulsion was based on sexual drives and primitive urges, which he labeled the pleasure principle.[1]

Over the years, many therapists have continued developing Freud's theory on the repetition compulsion, one of whom was Scottish psychoanalyst Ronald Fairbairn. He deviated from Freud's ideas on love and sexual drives in the repetition compulsion,[xv] believing people desired

---

[1] Pleasure principle: Humans have an instinctive drive to pursue pleasure and avoid pain.

to feel emotionally connected to an other rather than just the desire to be desired. He saw a hermeneutic component of loss and gain and came to the conclusion that we need to lose someone or something so that we can try to regain it, only to lose it again and try to regain it again, and so on and so forth. His contribution to the theory forces people to come to terms with impossibility, meaning, we can't always get what we want. Fairbairn's emphasis on impossibility and the grief that accompanies it is then accepted by Winnicott, who developed the theory even more. Winnicott adds an emphasis on play and possibility with impossibility, meaning, once you understand that you can't always get what you want, you can get what you need, which ultimately is what you want.

When two people in a relationship begin to understand what they are acting out with each other and have empathy for it without needing to fix it, then there is a good enough connection with the other or lover, just as there needed to be but wasn't with the (m)other. This is how people can move past their pain and into possibility. It's how they start to recalibrate their internal compass and relationship maps (which will be discussed more in part 2).

Alice Miller continued to emphasize grieving the past in her book, *The Drama of the Gifted Child*. She knew that when people grieve, not just cognitively understand, but actually grieve and feel the pain of the lost possibilities of their childhoods, then and only then can they learn how to find what they want and need in their adult relationships. This is much easier said than done. Grieving, which will be discussed more in part 3, is a process that many understandably avoid. Nobody likes to feel pain. Yet if people understood the internal reward that comes when people grieve a loss (a recalibrated internal map and compass that allows for better relationships), I bet more would embrace the process.

Just as athletes know that they can't win every game, but they can have a winning season if they learn from their losses, so can adults in their relationships. It's how they can turn their inner crisis of starting over into playing a game that always requires practice and can be a lot of fun. They make it through midseason when they learn to play with the paradox of impossibility and impossibility (e.g., when old wounds from the past get triggered in the present by things their partners do, they know this wound is theirs to grieve and not someone else's to take care of). They also have empathy for the other when their stuff gets acted out. When couples consistently practice these relational wind sprints, (own what's theirs and have empathy for what's not) their internal compasses continue to get recalibrated and relationship maps recreated. They begin to move in a positive direction, season after season, year after year. These wind sprints, which therapists call creative repetitions, will be discussed in part 3, as well.

The goal of therapy for both Ted and Jenny was to help them heal their inner childhood wounds, which in turn would create a secure inner attachment. They needed to do this first, before either of them could learn how to have committed, authentic, playful, passionate, and compassionate relationships, with many winning seasons. Once I explained that to them, they understood the rules of the game. They found the hope they needed inside to help them get back out there and play. This next story was written for them.

Feature Story: Can Every Day Be an Opening Day
in Your Relationship?

Oh, put me in coach, I'm ready to play today.
—John Fogerty

Opening Day began with a bang this year. Tom Brady threw out the first pitch. Rob Gronkowski playfully stole his Super Bowl LI jersey. The pair chased each other cat-and-mouse style all the way to shallow right field. And most importantly, the Red Sox won.

It doesn't get much better than that, in sports and in love. Yet many people find themselves lost in the field of disillusionment when the excitement of Opening Day (courting phase) with their partner wears off. Not knowing if they can end their losing streak, they agonize over whether or not their love can last. They wish every day could be Opening Day. In every relationship, there really is only one Opening Day: when people first become infatuated with each other. However, if a couple can come to understand some basic plays in the field of love, then it's very possible, should they have both the will and desire, to have many winning seasons together. So what are some of those basic plays?

1. *First, understand your attachment style*: How you were loved when you were young is how you love as an adult. Some people need to feel close all the time; others need more space, and some feel anxious, ambivalent, or even avoidant when there is too much or too little of either one. Most people are drawn to others whose attachment style feels in sync with their own.

2. *Heal your inner attachment.* Those who have a secure inner attachment and got just the right amount of closeness and space as a child tend to fare better in long-term relationships. Those who didn't get enough of what they needed often put the responsibility on the other to somehow make up for it. That's when the fighting and disillusionment begin. Remember that you are the only person who can make up for it.

3. *Know that it's not possible for one person to fulfill 100 percent of what you need all the time.* The other person will eventually fall off the pedestal and let you down. When couples learn to recover from the errors in play they both make, they become better teammates. Learning to give yourself what you need and getting back up after you fall down time and time again makes winning together possible.

4. *Honestly assess your willingness to continue playing*: Sometimes, people outgrow each other. Not all relationships last through the seasons of a lifetime. Many couples stagnate as they experience their ambivalence about staying together. Some work through it and rediscover their Opening Day excitement and commitment to playing through this season and the next. Others decide it's better to leave or even switch teams.

5. *Find the courage to know and do what's right for you.* The rules of dating, mating, and relating are changing as serial monogamy and even polyamory (an open relationship) have become the new, albeit minor league, options in town. They're not for everyone, but they do offer viable options for some.

Now that Opening Day has come and gone, let's see if the Sox have what it takes to earn a winning season. And if your Opening Day has come and gone, then you'll soon discover that too. Regardless, play on.

Color Commentary

Psychologist James J. Lynch, author of *A Cry Unheard: New Insights into the Medical Consequences of Loneliness*, has spent his career researching the connection between human loneliness and premature death caused by heart attacks. He's not only made the case for such; he's gone further in proving Freud's revelatory idea that psychic pain becomes physical pain, and this pain can also lead to an early demise. Lynch states, "It's a striking fact that U.S. mortality rates for all causes of death, and not just heart disease, are consistently higher at all ages for divorced, single, and widowed individuals of both sexes and all races."[xvi] He also makes note that the idea "better off wed then dead"[xvii] is not the secret to living a long and happy life, asserting that the level of emotional satisfaction in a marriage (or lack thereof) can be a contributing factor leading to heart attacks and other medical conditions that cause premature death as well.

With that said, some partnerships consistently have poor health and losing seasons, no matter how much they practice their relational skills or how hard they try. When this happens, more often than not, only one member of the team is sincerely trying to make things work. The other may give the appearance of trying, but only so they don't lose the one who is. Thus, a different kind of relational crisis in love's labor's lost arises, one that involves trying to survive and change an abusive or manipulative partner.

CHAPTER 3

Manipulative Partners and Abuse: How These Crises Happen and How to Survive Them

> You just keep on pushing my love over the borderline.
> —Madonna, *"Borderline"*

To *manipulate* means "to manage or influence skillfully, especially in an unfair manner" or "to adapt or change to suit one's purpose or advantage." Most of us have used this tactic once or twice in our lifetime to get something we wanted, as directly asking probably wouldn't have worked, but later we feel guilty about it. For some, though, manipulating is a way of being. It's how they operate and even survive in the world. Trying to negotiate a relationship with this type of partner can feel almost impossible.

That's because it is.

Almost is the key word, though, because the one doing the manipulating needs to keep the other in the game and will occasionally throw them a bone of hope, making things feel almost possible.

Charlie Brown and Lucy van Pelt[xviii]

There's a scene from the *Peanuts* comic strip between Charlie Brown and Lucy van Pelt that illustrates this dynamic. Charlie desperately wants to kick the football that Lucy has, so she offers to let him, but just when he's about to kick it, she pulls it away. Then she promises again to let him kick it; he becomes hopeful and excited that he will finally get to kick it, but guess what? Just when he's about to kick it, she pulls it away from him, yet again. His continued experience of humiliation makes way for her continued sense of power and control, with the added benefit of sadistic pleasure. Until Charlie sees it for what it is, he will keep trying to kick that football. But he will never kick the football, and the sooner he realizes that, the sooner he can wiggle his way out of this dynamic. If you find yourself in Charlie Brown's shoes, you are not alone.

Marilyn felt trapped in web of torturous dynamics with her partner. Everything in their world revolved around him and his needs. When she would ask for things she wanted, he would either conveniently forget or make some kind of excuse for why he couldn't follow through. When she would express her disappointment, he would tell her she was overreacting and found a way to twist his neglectful and thoughtless behavior into somehow being her fault. A day never went by without him criticizing or belittling her. Her self-esteem slowly eroded, and she began to isolate herself from her friends.

Despite being unable to have a winning season with him, Marilyn was determined to make that possible. "It wasn't always this way," she would say. "He used to be so thoughtful and sweet." With enough therapy and self-help, she believed their record could go from worst to first, and they could somehow get their opening day back, but it never did. After she realized his character, she tried to leave him a couple of times. Yet just before she was out the door, she always seemed to get sucked back in. "I want to give it a little more time before I leave," she would say. "I have to know 100 percent in my heart that leaving is the right thing to do, before I go."

Struggling with traumatic symptoms ranging from panic to numbness, Marilyn looked at me one day and said, "I feel like I've been raped over and over again, but I wasn't."

"That makes perfect sense," I responded, "because from my perspective, your heart was."

Unbeknownst to Marilyn, she had an implicit contract with her partner, one where she somehow became his emotional punching bag.

Brian found himself in a different kind of implicit contract with his partner, Ben, struggling to understand why things always went sour. "He makes me feel crazy inside," he told me, "and sometimes I lose my cool. I am genuinely a mild-mannered guy, but not with him. We have this incredibly intense and loving connection, and then he turns on a dime and is nasty toward me. I wonder if he's bipolar."

Brian's need to analyze and try to understand Ben's erratic behavior went on for months. Tormented by Ben's treatment of him, along with his excessive drinking and occasional infidelity, Brian had come to his wit's end. That end just always seemed to have a new beginning, though. For years, Brian agonized over why trying to leave Ben felt just as hard as staying.

Lore also had a complicated relationship with his wife. Per his description of her in therapy, she was always hysterical about something that she needed him to take care of. He felt exhausted by her neediness, constantly complained about body aches and pains, and noticed that his desire for her had faded. His implicit contract with her looked much different from Brian and Marilyn's. He found himself feeling emotionally disconnected from his wife, who constantly begged him for his affection and attention. Sensing he was always one foot out the door and not emotionally satisfied in the marriage, she always manufactured some kind of crisis, health, financial, or emotional, to keep him hooked in her emotional dependency. He felt guilty when he wanted to leave; her pleas, cries, and threats of emotional blackmail would lure him back in, as he feared her warning that he'd "screw up the kids" if he left her.

These scenarios hit home with many, who find themselves scratching their heads with bewilderment, wondering how this all happened. While more common than most are prepared to admit, being involved with a manipulative or abusive partner comes with some challenging relational dynamics.

Drive-Ins, Relationship Maps, and Imago

In the good old days of drive-in movies, long before Lowes, Showcase Cinemas, On Demand, or Netflix came into being, advertisers relied on a technique to get people to buy their food and snacks. Either before the movie or during intermission, when trailers of other films played, a tiny flash frame of popcorn, soda, and candy would be inserted into the film. This frame couldn't be seen by the untrained eye. The strategy worked, though, and people found themselves magnetically drawn to the concession stand. The same sort of thing happens in relationships when people's relationship maps gets activated; they feel themselves magnetically pulled toward someone. Some call this love at first sight.

Imago[2] work, developed by Dr. Harville Hendrex and Dr. Helen LaKelly Hunt, explains more how relationship maps get turned on. In a nutshell, the magnetic pull that you feel toward another has much to do with implicit memories developed during your attachment phase. It gets triggered, much like the subliminal flash frames in the drive-in, when you meet someone who subconsciously reminds you of what's familiar. The pull toward the other's concession stand of love can feel absolutely irresistible.

Rooted in the neuronal coding of the implicit memories formed in early childhood development, the pull and bond that Marilyn, Brian, and Lore had toward their partners was powerful. It was even more so when they would try to leave. Much like a hurricane that loses its strength when it hits land, anytime Marilyn, Brian, or Lore would set their intentions to get out of their relationships, they somehow found themselves back in the storm. The strength of this storm and magnetic pull toward their partner became more energized, taking them back out to sea. With land almost out of sight and a riptide pulling them even farther out into the open waters of the deep ocean, they knew they needed to find a different way back to shore.

They engaged in individual therapy, which taught them why they couldn't prevent the hurricane or shouldn't try to swim against the riptide of these kinds of relationships. It also taught them how to batten down the hatches, swim away from the riptide rather than against it, and eventually get out of the storm all together. It taught them that their wants and needs mattered and showed them how to start prioritizing.

---

[2] *Imago* means an unconscious, idealized mental image of someone that influences behavior. Hendrex and Hunt have written two books: *Getting the Love You Want* and *Keeping the Love You Find*, which detail how this kind of therapy works for couples.

It proved helpful for Marilyn, Brian, and Lore to learn more about both their and their partner's attachment styles, which wrote the scripts for their current relational contracts. In time, and with a constant but gentle redirection in therapy to turn the focus back on themselves, they healed their inner attachments from insecure to secure (see chapter 2). While all three began therapy wanting to fix their partner, in time, therapy helped them learn to prioritize their own wants and needs, while having compassion for the part of them that had a tendency to put the other first. In essence, they came to discover how they were reenacting their childhood traumas, either the direct abuse or neglect they experienced from their parents or witnessing abusive or neglectful behaviors their parents acted out which each other, which is a scary thing for a child to take in. This became the unconscious code in their relationship map, which directed them toward allowing themselves to be neglected and abused later on in life.

Many who find themselves in same situations as Marilyn, Brian, or Lore report feeling utterly confused when they come to terms with their own attachment style. They wonder if they have an insecure attachment that draws them toward this kind of person and keeps them there, even when they know they should leave; why, they ask, don't they act like them? The answer is, the ruptures in their attachment happened later in their own childhood development than their partners'. The nonmanipulative partner got to develop more of a sense of self.

Though most of the research on attachment and object relations focuses on the first few years of life, ruptures later in childhood and adolescent development can affect your internal compass and relationship map too.

Manipulative or abusive partners tend not to be so curious about their significant other. It's often because they've had severe neglect or trauma early in their development, before they could even speak. It's so deeply woven into their sense of self that they don't see their behavior as manipulative. On some level, they are developmentally the age of the rupture, which is cognitively too young to have insight or think of other people's wants and needs. Like a needle skipping across a record, they constantly travel down this undeveloped and undrawn direction in their relationship map, acting out the rupture imprinted on it.

The types of insecure attachments the partners of Marilyn, Brian, and Lore developed varied in presentation. Marilyn's husband had a narcissistic style. Brian's partner had a borderline style, and Lore's wife displayed histrionics and dependence.[3] And yes, truth be told, we all have an inner narcissist, borderline, dependent, and histrionic tendencies. That's what being human is all about. Here's a deeper explanation of those styles:

Narcissism and the Myth of Narcissus

Let's start with narcissism. Remember the Greek myth of Narcissus? Yes, we are back in ancient Greece again. He was the handsome rock star of Athens; everyone idolized him. According to the myth, though everyone loved him, no one measured up to his standards. One day, while riding his horse through the woods, he saw his reflection in the pond and found the one person who did. In his desire to be closer to this love, he fell into the pond and drowned.

I once heard a therapist tell a different version of the myth. Yes, Narcissus is still the rock star in Greece, and everyone still idolizes him, but no one really knows him or loves him for anything other than his appearance and rock star status. Inside, he is lonely, longing for a connection that he's never had. One day, while riding through the woods on his horse, he sees his reflection in the pond. At last, he believes, he has found someone who really knows him and loves him for who he is. In his desire to obtain that love, which is with himself, he falls into the pond and drowns. This is obviously a more empathic view, one which is needed in therapy for those with narcissistic styles.

Narcissism is an expression of neglect. There is little parental attunement with the child's needs during the first five years of life, including a lack of behavioral limits; therefore, a sense of emptiness and entitlement manifests. "I want what I want" becomes the modus operandi (MO) for these children, as acting out and bullying become the best ways

---

[3] Here's a brief description of the above attachment styles. *Narcissism*: It's all about me. *Borderline*: I need you to be me, so please don't leave me. If you do, I will turn from Dr. Jekyll to Mr. Hyde. *Histrionic*: A combination of the two, with a flair for drama.

to can get attention or connection. "I have to get what I want" becomes the motto for the adult, believing that thing will fill up their inner void. What they want is attention, admiration, and love, but it's never enough, and they don't know how to reciprocate. They do, however, figure out how to give their partner just enough of what she or he needs, quid pro quo style, so they can get their needs met. They get the better end of the deal, though. Partners become objects to obtain, neglect, torment, and abuse, something they feel completely entitled to do. This is so because it's what happened to them, and it's all they know.

Borderline Styles

Rupture, repair, rupture, repair, and once again rupture, repair. Those with borderline styles constantly feel injured and abandoned; working with them in therapy can be challenging. They require constant repair from perceived injuries and abandonment. It's also why these kinds of romantic partnerships feel so draining.

Psychoanalyst Melanie Klein and psychoanalyst and physician Margaret Mahler, both of whom were born in the late 1800s, circa the time Freud was studying hysteria in France (Klein was actually a few years prior to this), wrote much about this, shaping our current understanding of borderline phenomenology. They were practicing therapy when women were the primary caregivers, staying at home with their children, and men were off working. The fault in these types of attachments back then inevitably falls upon the mother. In an effort to steer away from mother bashing and acknowledge that modern parenting has changed since Mahler and Klein developed their ideas, it's worth saying that these days, fathers, mothers, grandparents, and nannies alike could all substitute for the role of mother if they were the primary caregiver. Therefore, I will present the M in "mother" in parentheses when explaining their ideas. Let's start first with Mahler, who focused on the stages and substages of development from infancy to approximately three years of age.

Mahler contended that as newborns merge with their (m)other,[xix] their senses of self do, as well. Sometime around five months, when they start to separate and individuate from their mother, which Mahler called "hatching," newborns begin to explore the world around them, always looking back though to see if their (m)other was still there. If the (m) other is there and lovingly attuned to the infant, it ensures infants their selves are there, as well. If their (m)others are there consistently during this phase, infants will feel safe enough to continue explore the world around them, and then returning to the safety of their (m)others' arms. Taking a couple of years, if this rapprochement process takes place with good enough (m)othering, children develop a separate sense of self. If there isn't good enough (m)othering, then their sense of self stays enmeshed with their (m)others. When the (m)other is not there, when the child looks back, distress and panic set in, since the (m)other is still the infant's sense of self. If this happens with great frequency during this phase, a rupture in the attachment is born that manifests as neediness, dependency, and an extreme fear of abandonment.

This trauma later gets reenacted when children become adults who form relationships with others. If the other tries to leave, it threatens their sense of identity, just as it did when they were children. The implicit memory of the abandonment gets triggered, and they will go to extreme measures to prevent their partner from leaving, as the loss poses an overwhelming threat to their very own identity, just as it did when they were children.

Melanie Klein, whose ideas were similar to Mahler's, focused more on something that Mahler wrote about, but Klein nailed it. It's called "projective identification," which has to do with a very specific kind of rupture in attachment during the separation and individuation phase of development. Remember when Brian said that Ben made him feel crazy inside and that sometimes he would lose his cool? That's an example of it. It's kind of like when someone dares you to hit them, but you say no. They persist, saying all kinds of mean and nasty things to hurt you and keep at it, until you reach your boiling point and succumb. If you do, then you've just aided and abetted them in a replay of their childhood trauma (which they need you to do) by taking on the role of their abuser. If, however, you don't do their bidding and decide to walk away, they could get hijacked by the pain of abandonment, which they cannot tolerate. Some will threaten or even attempt suicide, and others will shame their partner or find a different Achilles' heel, one that is theirs and theirs alone. When trapped in the web of this type of dynamic, it often feels like you are damned if you do and damned if you don't.

Klein contended that this type of behavior mirrors what the caregiver was doing to the child during their separation and individuation phase. The best way to get a picture of what this looks like is to remember *Sybil*, a book written by Flora Rheta Schreiber and then turned into a movie starring Sally Fields. Though Sybil had dissociative identity disorder (commonly known as multiple personalities), someone with borderline pathology had a (m)other who to some degree, though not as extreme, behaved like Sybil's mother did. And Sybil's (m)other had a (m)other who did the same to her. It's a generational legacy, mirroring the ancestral legacy of Venus and Psyche (see chapter 1) of mother-daughter as well as parent-child trauma that ends when the child gets just enough consistent love and attunement from someone in their early developmental sphere. This creates some sense of a separate sense of self, enough of which will bring them into therapy so they can develop it further. Therapy helps to end this legacy of trauma.

Histrionic, Dependent, and Sociopathic Styles

Histrionic and dependent styles blend the best of both narcissistic and borderline attachments, making these kinds of relationships feel beyond confusing. Lore also described his wife as being very sweet at times, making his favorite meals and buying theater tickets to his favorite shows. Parts of her did love him, just as parts of him did love her. This added to his guilt, the hook she played on, when he longed to leave. Learning to trust one's confusion as a clue that something isn't quite right is the key to healing from these kinds of relationships.

Last but not least, there's the sociopath. I'm not necessarily talking about Ted Bundy or Jeffrey Dahmer, but they do fit the profile. Instead, there's a type a person, a con artist, who brilliantly feigns empathy and seems to offer the perfect connection of love, attention, and bliss, only later to rob their partner blind and take them for all they have. Bruce Perry brilliantly captures the origins of sociopathy in his book *The Boy Who Was Raised as a Dog: And Other Stories from a Child Psychiatrist's Notebook: What Traumatized Children Can Teach Us About Loss, Love and Healing*. A master in parroting civilized human behavior, this[xx] person is all smoke and mirrors. If you see past their illusion, they will be none too happy, as they need to believe their own lies. The threat posed to their deluded sense of self if you dare to see past them will then pose a threat to you. Remember Bowlby's experience of watching baby goslings attach to their mother? If they didn't form that attachment during a certain window of time, then they didn't attach at all. The same principle holds true for sociopaths. They have no attachment, and when you really think about it, that's a tragedy. They were robbed of something so basic and vital, and in turn, they act this out by robbing you, just the same.

One final note and confession, though, before you read on. I used the world *style* rather than disorder for a reason, as I absolutely hate calling someone manipulative, narcissist, borderline, codependent, depended, histrionic, or any other label you can imagine. I did so, however, on purpose.

The capacity for humans to grow, heal, and change, regardless of what cards they got dealt, is as infinite and unbound as all the stars in the Milky Way and the universe itself, provided one has an honest will and desire for it. The road to wellness is usually long and challenging, filled with hurdles and setbacks. Also, a person's will and desire may be only partially genuine, another hook to keep the other by their side. But it would be unfair to say it's impossible. I've worked with many borderline and narcissistic clients over the years who did have a genuine desire to heal. They did the work, and in time, they did heal.

Labels, however, serve a purpose, one of which I was not forthright with. It gives you, the reader and witness to Marilyn, Brian, and Lore's stories, which fortunately did not include any physical violence, a sense of space from this type of person you may be involved with. And for those who think they may feel stuck in the implicit contract of this kind of relationship, space is exactly what they need.

This next story grew out of a moment of countertransference I was having (which is therapist vernacular for being overly involved with a client's story) with a client who was very stuck in her denial with a manipulative and emotionally abusive partner. Not really on my game during this particular session, my crass and unconventional response did become an unexpected game changer for her.

Feature Story: Implicit Contracts

You're so vain, you probably think this song is about you.
—Carly Simon

Narcissistic abuse has become a hot talking point these days. If you follow social media, particularly Facebook, you may find many articles about how to spot a narcissist, gaslighting (a manipulative technique where your partner tries to convince you that you are crazy and are imagining their abuse rather than take any responsibility for it), and signs that your partner is a psychopath. While these essays do have some meat to them and offer sound advice on self-care, such as trusting your instincts and maintaining no contact once you end the relationship, they don't get to the heart of the matter, which is why people get ensnared in these relationships in the first place.

Karen had been in therapy with me for two years. Her husband, Jack, who was once the love of her life, had been showing her his darker side for many years. He often neglected her, raged at her when he was upset, and seldom showed any genuine interest in Karen's wants and needs. When she would withdraw her attention from him and begin to contemplate leaving the relationship, he would then change his tune and start following through on the many promises he made to her. This, in turn, offered her some intermittent moments of hope and happiness, and she would re-engage with him. Yet once she did, little by little, he would switch back to his old behaviors. After a while, she would then start to withdraw again, and he would start to pursue her again. He offered her just enough of what she needed to get her hooked into riding the roller coaster of his moods and maltreatment. This was their relational contract.

The contract didn't start out that way, though, and generally speaking, in this kind of relationship, it never does. Karen told me that she and Jack were once very much in love.

"We had a chemistry like no other, and he always felt like my soulmate," she would say, which I am sure was true.

This kind of chemistry, however, allowed for the classic bait and switch where, over time and unbeknownst to her, she came to implicitly agree to be in a connection with him that ultimately was all about him. Never did she imagine herself to be a sounding board for his dreams and disappointments and a psychic punching bag for his rage. Always trying to fix him or therapize him, she lived with chronic knots in her stomach. Obsessed with how to get things back to the way they used to be, she came to therapy after her friends and family expressed concerns on how her self-confidence and joie de vivre seemed lost. She agreed that it was.

So how did this implicit contract get signed?

Karen grew up in a disorganized household. Her father, who adored her, traveled for work, so he wasn't around much of the time, and her mother, who was a trauma survivor herself, would often rage at Karen when she was a little girl. Karen shared with me her memory of her mother screaming at her for some unknown reason, as she didn't remember doing anything wrong. Her mother's affect was so intense that Karen remembered wanting to faint in an attempt to get her to stop and to win back her mother's love. "I just wanted her to hold me," she said as she wept silent tears.

As a four-year-old, Karen did not know how to stand up for herself; she couldn't run away. Those are not skills that any small child has. Instead, she developed a belief that it was her job to take care of her mother's emotional needs. By doing this job, which was necessary for her own sense of survival, she denied her burdens, ignoring her own feelings of fright, anger, loneliness, and abandonment that arose during and after her mother's tirades. When she was older and did try to protect herself, her actions were then met with more rage and more neglect. In many ways, her relational wings were clipped.

So how did this type of trauma manifest in Karen's intrapsychic system? First, she developed panic and fainting disorders, as her fight-or-flight response lived in constant overdrive for many years. Second, she found herself in a string of bad relationships, until she met her husband (or so she thought).

A couple of days before I had a session with Karen, I learned that a former client I treated for many years when working at a methadone clinic had overdosed and died. He too grew up in an extremely disorganized household. He was from Medford, Massachusetts, or as many homegrown Beantowners prefer to say, "Medfa." A talented artist who dropped out of school because of drugs, he knew how to stand his ground, and he never back down from a fight, even when he probably should have. Unlike Karen, who didn't know what to say when her husband mistreated her, my former client had just the perfect vernacular of hysterically funny and vulgar pushback lines for when someone mistreated him.

He was on my mind during a session with Karen, which ended up being a turning point in the therapy. She was trying to find a way to stand up for herself in anticipation of her husband's next outburst. I began to tune out as she practiced and played with polite niceties such as "When you do that, I feel … [blah blah blah]." Then suddenly, I got hijacked by intense countertransference and interrupted her.

I said, just as my former client would have, "No, the next time he acts out, you tell him to go choke on a big fat d--k."

Silence filled the room.

Then a spontaneous eruption of laughter between the two of us took up the space and remained there for the rest of the session.

My former client would have been very proud. Karen took his lead and said something to that nature to her husband a few day later when he started up again. It worked. Stunned by both her words and assertiveness, he apologized and told her that she was right, he did need to go back to therapy.

Whether or not Karen's husband can earnestly engage in treatment and learn to become more relational remains to be seen. His declaration could be yet another bait-and-switch move, where he offers her just enough of something that appeases her so that she'll get back on the roller coaster with him because he can't tolerate losing her. In narcissistic alliances, however, the loss has little to do with the loss of the actual person. It's more about the loss of an object that supplies the other with a drug-like fix. If a person does leave the alliance, the other may quickly find another empathic partner who will take the previous one's place.

These alliances are not always so black and white, though. Some people can have a continuum of relationality. They may both genuinely care for the other and see them as an object at the same time. This is when it gets really confusing. Where the person is on the narcissistic continuum will be the deciding factor on whether this relational dynamic can change or not. That is why therapy is a must to survive something of this nature.

Karen and Jack need to enter couples counseling, if they want to remain in their relationship; if they do, they may be in constant contract negotiations for a long time (provided Jack is honest and forthcoming in the therapy).

Yet there's a creative genius behind Karen's relational patterns. When she was four years old, she was frightened, angry, lonely, and abandoned; parts of her got pushed aside when dealing with her mother's abuse. For years, these parts kept desperately trying to find ways to have their story seen and heard, by none other than Karen herself. One of their tactics was to find just the perfect partner to contract with who would help them reenact their story. They are the parts of her (and of you, for that matter, if you can relate to Karen's story) who signed the implicit contract in the first place.

The good news is, once you see what these parts are up to, you can then take a front row seat to their show, just as Karen did. With a little curiosity and a lot of compassion, which allows these injured parts to grieve and heal in their own time and space, you'll be able to rip up that contract and get off the roller coaster for good. And if you start to waffle when your partner makes a desperate attempt to lure you back in, try imagining yourself saying the crass words of my former client: "Go suck on a big fat d--k." Allow that energy to fill your body with courage. Next, take a long, slow deep breath, find some stillness, and pause. Then calmly look your partner in the eye and say just one word:

Goodbye.

Color Commentary

Women and men alike manipulate and abuse each other. Yet when Hollywood makes a film commenting on this, as in *Fatal Attraction*, they show the woman as the perpetrator and man as the victim. According to the National Coalition against Domestic Violence, the scale tips in the other direction. Women in the United States share a greater statistical percentage as the injured party than men do. According to their data, one in seven women (19.3 million) and one in eighteen men (5.1 million) have been stalked by an intimate partner. One in four women and one in seven men have been victims of severe physical violence by an intimate partner. One in five women and one in seven men have been raped in their life time. Women between the ages of eighteen and twenty-four are most commonly abused by an intimate partner, and in 72 percent of all murder-suicides involving an intimate partner, 94 percent of the victims are female.[4]

As a rule, I don't tell people whether they should stay or go when they are involved with a manipulative or abusive partner, although I will express my concern. I believe it's important to respect clients' process and autonomy, while giving them safety resources they may need. The decision to leave an abusive or manipulative partner is the client's decision to make, one they must make for themselves, not for me or anyone else. If I have an agenda to get someone to leave this kind of crisis, even though I may believe it's what's in their best interest, it can do more harm than good. It may shame those who want to stay or just aren't ready to go, which could cause them to leave the therapy prematurely or not really talk about what's at stake.

This same principle holds true for those who are struggling with another crisis of love's labor's lost: infidelity.

---

[4] http://www.ncadv.org

CHAPTER 4

Understanding Infidelity: Easing the Pain of Betrayal through Harm Reduction

I know that it's a secret and that I have to keep it.
—Meiko

"If he cheated on her, he will cheat on you," Ella said to Betty during the weekly Thursday night's women's group, offering her advice and support. Betty, a fifty-four-year-old divorcée, had begun an emotional affair with her longtime friend and was considering taking it to the next level. She knew her friend was contemplating leaving his marriage, and the two were becoming closer by the hour. Nonetheless, she felt tormented over the thought of engaging in something that went against her values. Upon sharing her dilemma, the group voiced their disapproval, sounding in agreement with Ella's fiery caution.

Betty's body grew tense. She clenched her jaw, held her breath, and began to shut down and grow quiet.

"What are you thinking?" Ella asked Betty, as she sensed she was holding something back.

"Do you really want to know?" Betty responded.

"Yes, of course," she said, and the group seemed open and curious too.

"All right," Betty said. "Ella, I know you are just looking out for me, and I appreciate that. I don't know whether or not he's a serial cheater, and I don't think it's fair that you assume that. Didn't you say once in the group that you had an affair during your first marriage?"

"Yes," Ella replied, "but it was during the 1970s, and it was a different time. Everyone was doing that. Plus, my first husband and I weren't really right for each other."

"I understand," Betty said. "My friend doesn't think he and his wife are right for each other either, and he says he's felt this way since before he married. But for argument's sake, let me ask you this: Would you cheat on your current husband?"

"No," Ella shot back. "Of course not. Never. He's the love of my life, and I am so grateful to have him."

Betty paused and looked at Ella, who seemed to now understand where Betty was coming from.

"You're right, Betty. Touché. Things aren't always so simple. But still, I don't like what you've told me about this guy, and I don't want you to get hurt."

I then chimed in, "It sounds like you both have something very important to say about affairs and infidelity; perhaps neither point of view is wrong or right."

They paused for a moment as they let that sentiment sink in. They both did have different yet valid ideas about affairs. As the therapist facilitating the group, I too found myself torn between feeling protective of Betty, knowing that she could get very hurt if she chose to get more involved with her friend, and wanting at the same time to respect Betty's autonomy so she could make whatever decision she wanted.

When I treated clients with addiction, one of the most powerful lessons I learned as a therapist was the importance of helping people explore their ambivalence around giving up their drinking and drug use, rather than insisting on total sobriety. The latter creates an unsafe space for clients to be truthful about their cravings and urges if they sensed disapproval on my end. They wouldn't be able to do the therapeutic work necessary to understand what was driving their behavior if they couldn't be honest and forthcoming.

I felt it necessary to apply that same principle here. The group needed to be kept safe so that Betty could talk about her desire to be with this man. The group's disapproval of her secret desire needed to be reconfigured into a compassionate expression of protectiveness, which also respected her right to make her own choices, no matter what they were. This way, members could continue to share their concerns with Betty in a loving way, and in turn, Betty would be able to really hear what they were saying. Should she decide to act on her desire, just as people with addiction do when they slip and relapse, she would then need to be able to talk about it in the group. Just as my addiction clients benefited from sharing their struggles, Betty needed that opportunity, as well.

Moralizing around behavior, which can be very hard not to do when that behavior causes others a lot of pain, keeps us from really understanding it. It reinforces the need for secrecy and perpetuates the cycle of shame and deception. Plus, human beings are paradoxical in nature. When they feel polarized over something, they both want and don't want to do it. Trying to tip the scale in the direction we think is best, without exploring both sides of the struggle, actually tips it in the other direction. Making the group safer and less judgmental allowed Betty to share how lonely she had been since her divorce. She was able to share and explore for herself why she was deeply drawn to her friend. The group then joined her in her pain, as other women shared their loneliness too; the therapy and discussion benefited everyone.

Creating safety and space for people to talk about the darker side of their humanity is not a vote of encouragement to act on it. Just as I would never tell my addiction clients to go out and drink or do drugs, I wouldn't encourage someone to engage in an affair, either. If there isn't freedom in a therapeutic setting for clients to explore their wants, needs, desires, and cravings, or talk about them when they act on them, that setting will inadvertently give those wants and needs more power and charge. Talking about them can actually help to discharge the charge and keep people from acting impulsively. It reduces harm.

Lessons from Harm Reduction

Affairs and infidelity involve an act of betrayal involving three people that affects all three and more. The pain they cause can destroy marriages and ruin peoples' lives and reputations. They almost always do harm. After years of experience in treating addiction, a basic principle I learned is harm reduction, which I now find applicable when helping people work through the shattering pain of infidelity.

Harm reduction is a treatment modality and philosophy that seeks to reduce the harmful consequences of risky behavior rather than try to stop it. It embraces realism. Having condoms available in public schools to help prevent teenage pregnancy and helping drug-dependent clients develop safety plans to help prevent an accidental overdose are examples of harm reduction. It accepts that teenagers, no matter how much they are encouraged to practice abstinence, will have sex. And adults, no matter how much education they are given about the negative consequences of drug use, will still use drugs. Infidelity, in my view, is one such risky behavior that has been around since the time marriage was invented. Remember the myth of Cupid and Psyche (see chapter 1)? In order to marry Psyche, Cupid makes a deal with Jupiter, the king of the gods, who's married to Juno, the goddess of love and marriage. Jupiter agreed to let Cupid marry Psyche as long as he was willing to help him seduce mortal females for his extramarital liaisons. That story was told thousands of years ago. Elements of it are still true today and will be so tomorrow.

Harm reduction does not mean encouragement. On the contrary, it helps the therapist form safe relationships with clients where they can say anything and, yes, do anything too. Regardless of who in the triangle is coming in for therapy—the one who's cheating, the one who's being cheated on, or the other—holding the principles of harm reduction and creating a curious environment where people can honestly explore what's happening inside of them, without telling them to stop their behavior, provides a way to really work through of this kind of crisis.

Let's start with the one who's been cheated on. Almost nothing is more painful than learning that your partner has been unfaithful. It takes time to move past the shock of it. One of the biggest mistakes I've made as a therapist has been to move too quickly into exploring the relational dynamics in the couple that broke down prior to the infidelity. It can be misinterpreted that somehow the cheating was their fault. It wasn't. People are responsible for the choices they make, including the choice they make to not to talk about the problems in the relationship before any cheating took place.

April came to see me when she learned her husband had an affair. Absolutely devastated by this, she didn't know how she'd go on. "How could he do this to me?" she would ask angrily. "He's been lying to me for years. How could I ever trust him again?" Then she'd collapse into tears. A few months into therapy, after the shock of what happened was starting to wear off, I asked April if she had been happy in the marriage. She paused for a moment and said, "No, not really. I knew there were problems. I just didn't know how to talk about them."

"Why do you think that is?" I asked.

Her body began to cave inward as she quavered softly, "I don't know."

As we further explored why it was hard for her to bring up the "Are we happy?" conversation with him, she discovered something that helped things shift for her. She realized that she didn't bring it up because she was afraid the answer would be "No, we aren't happy."

"And if that were true," I added, "the two of you talked, and you both agreed you were unhappy, what do you imagine? What are you most afraid would come from that?"

Afraid of the marriage ending and being alone, April then realized that her silence served a purpose. I then asked her the following: "Have you ever thought that this person may no longer be right for you?" She suddenly perked up and seemed to feel more empowered.

I then asked her, "If you did end up alone, what are you afraid that might mean about you?"

She then started cry. "That would mean that something's wrong with me and no one will ever love me."

I explained to April that this was a belief she developed a long time ago that seemed true at the time but actually wasn't. She then became curious about her situation rather than feeling helpless from it. April found a little drop of hope.

By no means does the above questioning mean that April and her husband will divorce. It just helped her discover that there was a breakdown between the two of them, and neither knew what to do. This is a common reason people cheat: a systemic breakdown between the couple that neither knows how to address, often because they are afraid of what might happen if they do. If the breakdown does not get talked about and doesn't resolve on its own, then it's really just a matter of time before someone ends up acting out.

The responsibility of the systemic breakdown between the couple falls on both people. This does not at all condone the behavior of the one who chose to break their commitment and cheat, which can inaccurately suggest the act of infidelity was somehow the faithful one's fault. It wasn't.

Viewing the crisis of affairs and infidelity as something that resulted from a breakdown in the couple's system can help take away some of the sting. It can also help people who've been cheated on sort through any ambivalence they may have around staying in the relationship. Sometimes, this crisis serves as a wake-up call for the couple, one that helps them reinvent their relationship and recommit to each other in a much deeper and more authentic way.

Moving on to people who cheated, the affair itself can be very difficult for them to talk about, as it's a taboo subject, loaded with shame and secrecy. Though some affairs are brief and shallow, many are not. Afraid of the moral outrage from family and friends, that fear often gets projected onto the therapist, which keeps clients from talking about what they did. That then results in therapists and clients alike only brushing upon the subject. It keeps the people who cheated from truly understanding what's driving their behavior. It also keeps clients from talking about the depth of affection they may have for the other and their desire to be with the other instead of the one they chose to commit to. Just as in addiction treatment, if there's too much of a push toward abstinence (meaning immediately give up the other and recommit to the marriage before the client is ready), then more often than not, the people who cheated won't talk about the other in therapy. They will just maintain the affair and go to great lengths to keep it hidden.

Collin came to see me when he found himself in that predicament. He had been married for fifteen years, and for the last year, he had been having an affair. He wanted to leave his wife and be with the other woman. His friends and family urged him to stay with his wife and try to work things out for the sake of the kids. While the people in his world had noble intentions, their push was driving him ever more into the arms of his lover.

I said what I usually say when people come to my office in this kind of predicament: "I don't know what's right for you. Only you know that.

Sometimes, you follow your heart and deal with the guilt. Sometimes, you stay and work things out. All I know is that it's probably best to look inside yourself first before you make a choice, so that when you do, you've made the right one for you."

That intervention helped Collin get still in his body and mind. He was a man in love, and whatever choice he made involved pain. Knowing he could take the time in therapy to learn to have compassion and curiosity for his struggle gave him a drop of hope too.

While there are plenty of cases of infidelity where the one who cheats falls in the "narcissistic, manipulative partner" category, always trying to fill their inner void with the next fix, those folks generally don't seek out therapy. Cheating is a part of their relational pattern. More often than not, though, the people who've been unfaithful and come to my office to try to understand why are truly tormented by their predicament. Ashamed of what they have done, how they feel, and what they want (which they feel utterly confused about), they find themselves in one of the most agonizing crises imaginable. It takes a lot of patience and compassion to get to the heart of the matter.

As for the other in the triangle, this person suffers too. Most others who come to see me had no intention of ever being a home-wrecker and never imagined they would find themselves acting out one of the oldest stories in the world. While there are exceptions to the rule, affairs almost never work out for the other, unless of course they are willing to settle for crumbs.

Amanda came to see me when she found herself in that boat. An Ivy League overachiever with a successful career, she was horrified that she took that kind of risk.

"I've always followed girl code," she told me, as she never intended to hurt another woman. "He told me he was leaving her, over and over again, but he's never come through for me."

Amanda, who will be revisited in part 3, learned through therapy that she was reenacting her childhood neglect by choosing an unavailable mate. The constant roller coaster ride of excitement, passion, and euphoria always cycled down for Amanda, into the lulls of depression, anger, and despair. It was only a matter of time before she fell off the ride into the pit of harrowing heartache.

Helping others explore why they got on that roller coaster and what pathways in their relationship map drove them to make that choice can lead to a lot of personal growth. Again, a harm reduction approach can be helpful here, as the other needs just as much compassion as the couple. While anyone looking from the outside in can see that it's in Amanda's best interest to end the affair, as her lover never really followed through for her, trying to get her to end it before she's ready will only result in her keeping it a secret and staying on that ride even longer. Offering others an always available safety net to fall into when they are ready to jump off the roller coaster ride, while respecting their choice to ride it for as long as they need to, will help them get off when they are ready (hopefully, before the crash).

When Desire Looks Elsewhere

Renown couples therapist Esther Perel, author of *Mating in Captivity* and *State of Affairs*, often writes about couples whose lives have been forever altered by infidelity. She offers a highly examined and cross-cultural perspective that deconstructs the history of love and marriage, which helps make talking about infidelity a little less scary.

Late in the twentieth century, Perel[xxi] wrote how marriage traditionally was an arrangement made by two families to protect and continue their lineage of wealth and property. It provided security and offspring but had little to do with romantic love. That was something sought outside the marriage, and it was a privilege reserved mostly for men. There was one small exception, though, which included wealthy married women who were romanced by male troubadours during the Middle Ages. Still, throughout history, men were implicitly allowed to have their cake and eat it too.

With changing times and greater gender and economic equality, ideas about love and marriage have changed. Many have had numerous sexual partners, romantic liaisons, and established careers before they say, "I do." When people do marry, love, passion, and romance are some of the basic requirements in their nuptial agreements. With that said, affairs are more rampant now than they have ever been, in part because as Perel often says in her talks, "love doesn't always live up to its promise.[xxii] She also warns, "Philandering is here to stay," and it seems to cause more emotional damage than ever before. "When marriage was an economic arrangement, infidelity threatened our economic security. Today marriage is a romantic arrangement, and it threatens our emotional security."[xxiii]

Stephen Mitchell writes in *Can Love Last?* about the contradictory nature of love and desire, arguing that love needs connection, predictability, and stability, while desire needs space, spontaneity, freedom, and novelty. Do some couples have both? Yes, but many don't; after years of marriage, they have difficulty recreating the love and desire they once had for each other. Their longings land elsewhere as they find themselves gazing into the eyes of another and then falling into their bed.

There are also times when systemic breakdowns or lost desire is not the cause of infidelity. Sometimes, a person comes along and wakes up lost parts of another's being and the latent desires their soul longs to express. People in this situation generally don't come to my office. Boris Pasternak's *Dr. Zhivago*, a novel later turned into Metro-Golden-Mayer's classic film,[xxiv] explains that exact story. As a man who loves his wife and the family they created together, Zhivago falls in love with Lara, his mistress, who he can't stay away from. Lara awakens the long-lost poet in him, inspiring him to write about the passions of love in a most dangerous time in communist Russia. These passions could destroy everything he knows and loves, including himself, but he can't deny them.

There are no easy answers to infidelity's crisis of love's labor's lost. There are only fearless questions to be asked, honest and compassionate explorations to be done, and authentic outcomes to be had. Without such, people will keep moving along the trajectory of duplicity and strengthening the development of a false self, needed to emotionally survive. Working through the crisis of an affair can allow for tremendous healing and personal growth. Therapy can help people take advantage of this crisis to explore their attachment style, their family model of relationships and marriage, and any possible reenactment they may be partaking in on behalf of an unhealed part of themselves. It's the road to developing a true self, the road toward change; in my view, it's the way to go. It's the path toward hope.

Without hope, people will continue to cheat in the love arena, just as they continue to cheat in the arena of professional sports.

Feature Story: Cheating in Sports and in Love

> I told my wife the truth. I told her I was seeing a
> psychiatrist. Then she told me the truth: that she was
> seeing a psychiatrist, two plumbers, and a bartender.
> —Rodney Dangerfield

Only the New York press would congratulate the New England Patriots' historic Super Bowl comeback victory with this headline: "How Cheat It Is." In today's highly competitive sports world, the collective fan-ship of "we" often deifies athletes when they make great plays and win the game, like Tom Brady and David Tyree (sorry, New Englanders; I know that still hurts) and, in turn, shuns them when they expose their mere mortality by making mistakes and losing. To this day, most Red Sox fans react with a palpable groan upon the mention of Bill Buckner (my apologies again). But what happens to fans and to ourselves if we discover that the team or the one we've pledged to be faithful to happens to play by a different set of rules than we do? What happens when someone we love breaks a rule or, better yet, gets caught in the oh-so-scandalous act of cheating?

Our vicarious love affair with sports is not so different from our personal love affairs. Cheating happens. It always has, and right or wrong, it always will. Some deny it. Some find ways to justify it. Then, of course, there are some who forever moralize over the cheating with an unyielding vitriol (Hello, New York) that doesn't allow for the much-needed exploration of why it happened in the first place. At least that's what I encounter in my clinical practice with individuals and couples struggling with the effects of infidelity.

In sports, the why has many answers. The pressure to be the best all the time, which isn't possible, gets to some. The career-ending consequences for not being the best all the time gets to others. There is danger in the game itself, where the justified fear and high probability of a career-ending injury looms over every athlete. Consider what happened to Wes Welker and Travis Roy, among others, and the very real existential threat (this game may be my last) that ups the ante in the choice to cheat. Then there are leaders with power in the system, who lack consistency and even common sense in their decision-making process, giving one athlete a two-game suspension for beating his spouse and another four games for an equipment violation.

In a system where the rules don't always seem fair, or even make sense, that also lacks a forum for honest questioning and real feedback, players may begin to play by rules that make sense to them. And rather than question the validity of a flawed paradigm, have a real conversation about what to do about it, or even show a note compassion for the inevitable expression of its worst, most stick to the black-and-white, business-as-usual way of being and throw mud at those who dare to defy it. This, in particular, applies to rival teams; from a psychological perspective, they represent either our partner or the other in the so-called love affair. Ironically, when our team, which is a projection and expression of ourselves, comes under the same scrutiny, it generally doesn't suffer through the same level of ire.

The same holds true in love. The idea that one person can satisfy our every need for love, sex, relationships, and marriage over the course of a lifetime sets us up for failure. This is not to say that monogamous relationships can't last and even continue to be pleasurable while they last, for as long as the couple chooses (which for some is a lifetime). What makes that so?

There are many factors, the first of which embraces the idea that no one person can give us all that we need. Is that an invitation to begin searching outside the relationship for the holy grail of love and desire? Not necessarily, though many do start there once the chemistry fades (which, by the way, it always does). Experts in the field of love and eroticism, including anthropologist Helen Fisher, author of *The Anatomy of Love: A Natural History of Mating, Marriage, and Why We Stray,* offer up many cultural, psychological, scientific, and phenomenological reasons why the euphoric high of romance dissipates after two years (at most) and what comes after that. Some couples find themselves feeling like best friends or roommates; others become estranged, fighting with each other for not being the promised be-all and end-all for all of eternity they were supposed to be. Some become exhausted from the demands of work, life, and family, which often leave little time to recapture or reinvent the desire that brought them together in the first place.

At this crucial juncture, many begin reenacting their unfinished childhood business, including the abuse or neglect from their primary caregivers as well as other baggage, in a noble but impossible attempt to get now from their partner what they missed out on during their early developmental years. Those who fall into this category first need to learn to give themselves what they didn't get, rather than seek to find it in another because the other will always let them down. For the rest, most experts in the field of love, sex, and relationships say that which we seek outside of ourselves, we need to first find within. Only then can an authentic decision be made about staying, straying or moving along.

I personally don't believe that making it until "death do us part" is an accurate marker of marital success.[5] People sometimes outgrow each other and decide to part ways. Some choose to stay together for the sake of the family and openly seek love and desire outside the marriage. Some choose to stray, as they may be unconsciously seeking a way out that they are either afraid to express or don't know how to say with words. I don't claim to know which solution is best or right, as it varies from person to person. I have seen infidelity cause some great pain and irreparable damage. I have also seen it offer couples a necessary wake-up call, forcing them to find a way to reinvent themselves, and they often do.

Rather than moralize over it, why not see it as invitation to explore the systemic breakdowns and existential crises that led to it in the first place?

---

[5] Esther Perel. Ted Talk, May 21, 2015.

Or better yet, why not have a fearless talk with your partner about just that: before initiating an affair, bravely sharing what's happening within yourself, including your level of desire for the other and lack thereof, willingness or lack of willingness to recreate it, without blaming or pointing fingers? Though it may feel scary to voice this, having this conversation before an affair may help save you from having a very painful one after. Besides, if your marriage or partnership can't survive this conversation, then it's safe to say that it probably won't survive over the long haul anyway. It's the cleaner and ideal way to do things, but alas, life isn't always ideal, and human behavior is invariably messy.

While the above ideas may offer a sigh of relief to some, they may also feel jarring and even blasphemous for others. They don't make a claim on one right strategy or solution and probably do little to soothe one's anxiety over the subject. I can't say that I know the answer or even if there is one; however, this I do believe: if our collective love and marriage fan-ship, much like our sports fan-ship, can't begin to ask honest questions and be open to diverse answers and creative solutions, then the shaming, blaming, and humiliating scars of infidelity will continue to perpetuate and pervade those enthusiasts who choose to play the game of modern love.

Let's try to change that game.

Color Commentary

While there's no hard data on what percentage of people in committed relationships cheat, Esther Perel reminds us of a few facts that show the male advantage in this phenomena, writing, "Until recently, marital fidelity and monogamy had nothing to do with love. It was a mainstay of Patriarchy imposed on women, to ensure patrimony and lineage." She also states that unattached women are far more likely to be the other in an adulterous love triangle than unattached men, who only agree to such when all they want is a part-time relationship. In this scenario, "the other woman is judged far more harshly than the cheating husband."[xxv]

While infidelity can be one of the most painful crises on the path of love's labor's lost, there's one more that can hurt even more: divorce. For some, it's the worst crisis imaginable, and it's the last to be explored in part

1 of this book. Nothing feels more devastating than when someone wants to leave and the other wants them to stay. It's a heartbreak that words can't describe. The house of cards has fallen, and it won't be rebuilt. Many in this situation feel as though they've lost hope forever. Except, here's the kicker: they haven't. They just need to know where to look so they can find it again.

CHAPTER 5

When Someone Wants to Leave: Rethinking Divorce

What failure? I had three successful marriages for three different developmental periods of my life.
—Margaret Mead

"We had a commitment," Judy shouted as she held back the tears her rage masked. "How could he betray that?"

Richard spoke about his loss differently: "I believe there's the person you raise your family with and then there's the person you ride off into the sunset with."

Judy and Richard both got dumped by their spouses at midlife. Having been left for another, which neither of them ever wished for, they both experienced the devastation and life-altering upheaval that happens when someone chooses to leave a long-term marriage. Their perspective on their experience, however, has shaped how they recovered from it. Richard has moved forward and is happy, and Judy still suffers.

History is loaded with scandal when people defy the cultural code of conduct and leave their spouse for another. Helen of Troy (originally Sparta) left Menelaus for Prince Paris. Marc Antony left his second wife, Octavia, for his longtime lover, Cleopatra, and Jason of the Argonauts left Medea, the woman who defied her country and gave up everything to help him capture the Golden Fleece and become his wife. Ten years later, he found a younger princess to shack up with.

The aftermath of their actions was far from pretty: Medea sought revenge on Jason by killing her children and his new bride-to-be, Greece waged war against Troy, and Rome went to war with Egypt. Once defeated, Marc Antony and Cleopatra killed themselves.

Would they make those same choices again if they knew what the consequences of their actions would be? With the exception of Jason, who most likely would have stayed with Medea for the sake of the kids and had his princess mistress on the side, I would venture to say that they would do it all again. Why?

Because love is a powerful drug, and people take all kinds of risks to have it.

When someone awakens the longings in your heart and stirs your soul in a way that no one has ever done before, everything else in your life becomes insignificant. The aphorism "A life without love is not worth living" becomes your daily "Om."

Never have I seen such agony when someone decides to leave and their partner doesn't want them to. Is it the right thing to do? Not necessarily. It's also not necessarily the wrong choice, either. And just as Judy and Richard view the act of leaving from different vantage points, their divide on this mirrors the cultural divide, as well.

I write this chapter with great trepidation, knowing my perspective might be perceived as encouragement. It's not. While I have observed that too many people look to upgrade their partners without first looking to upgrade themselves or improve their partnership, at the same time, I've also observed that others stay in their marriage or partnership long past its expiration date. Like Newland Archer in *The Age of Innocence,* they end up living quiet lives of desperation for the sake of their children or fear the fallout that leaving will have. It's an understandable fear, especially when we consider historically what happens when people make this choice.

Forgotten Facts

But let's consider something else. At one time, everyone believed the world was flat. They also believed the sun revolved around the Earth, and that evolution was bunk. They were wrong. They argued vehemently against those new novel ideas (when it comes to evolution, some still do).

Embracing new paradigms about love, marriage, and partnership, just as Richard did, is a scary notion at first, more so for women who have embraced traditional roles and take care of the home and children, which Judy did. It is, however, the key to surviving and then later thriving after someone leaves. Just as infidelity is here to stay, so is trading partners. Though this may sound cynical, it's not meant to be so at all. It's written from the same harm reductionist point of view from the last chapter on infidelity, to help people come to terms with certain realities, so they don't feel so traumatizing if they do happen.

Cultural anthropologist Helen Fisher, author of *Anatomy of Love: A Natural History of Mating, Marriage, and Why We Stray,* has much to say on this subject. At one time, monogamy meant one person for life. Now, with divorce rates in the West at over 50 percent, coupled with changes in social and financial status that allow women almost the same freedoms as men, more and more people are changing partners after taking their nuptial vows. Fisher says that in today's modern world, most people will have two to three significant relationships in their lifetime.

When we consider the history of marriage, which had little to do with love and that "until death do us part" is a much longer time period these days than before, with people living well into their eighties and beyond, Fisher's data makes a lot of sense. This does not mean that people can't be happy with one partner for a lifetime, either. They can. There are just many truths when it come to the paradoxical nature of love. What's good for the goose isn't necessarily good for the gander. When a culture or a partner forces their paradigm onto another, who has different ideas, wants, and needs, in the long run, nothing good comes from it. It's death to the other. As Sting once famously sang, if you love someone who wants to leave, set them free.

That's much easier said and sung by a famous and wealthy rock star than done by the average Mary or Joe.

Gender Differences for Women in Divorce

There are sound reasons why Judy had a much tougher time getting past her loss than Richard did. Some are related to cultural conditioning, where young girls are spoon-fed fairy tales of a prince charming who will be their be-all and end-all forever. When these girls grow into women, they've been groomed to invest their self-worth and very lives into that of their husband. He (and yes, I'm speaking of heterosexual marriages here, though the cultural politics of gender affect same-sex marriages as well) becomes her sense of self. If he leaves, she loses both him and her identity. This is what happened with Judy.

A biology major in college, who excelled in her academic studies, Judy was on a premed track when she discovered she was pregnant. She dropped out of school to take care of her newborn, and her boyfriend, wanting to be a responsible father, married her. They then had three more children. Her husband, who was able to finish college, became the breadwinner in the family and enjoyed climbing the corporate ladder. She became a homemaker. She organized and managed all the household chores, made the meals, and handled the drop-offs and pick-ups for her kids' school and sporting events. Over the years, Judy and her husband grew apart. She noticed he was spending longer hours at work and didn't spend as much time with her. When the kids were grown, seemingly out of the blue, he told her he was leaving. Shell-shocked, she came to therapy. Hoping at first that she could win him back, depression began to sink in when she realized that wasn't going to happen.

"It's not fair," she cried. "I gave up everything for him."

Color Commentary

Inequitable gender dynamics, combined with complicated cultural biases, makes leaving tough on both people. Add an insecure attachment style in the partner who's being left to the mix, then the perfect storm of acrimonious uncoupling inevitably hits. The loss is just too devastating for the one being left, as it floods them with the implicit childhood memories of abandonment. The terror they felt when they were helpless and had little say in their parents' behavior comes back to life and overwhelms them. They often then will go to extremes to prevent being abandoned again. That's what the partners of Brian and Lore (see chapter 3) did. Each time Brian or Lore tried to break things off, emotional blackmail would force them to think twice. Brian's partner, Ben, who said he "would do anything" to save their marriage, threatened to kill himself if Brian left, and Lore's wife would threaten him with the fear of the damage leaving would do to their children.

Leaving does hurt the children. Lore's fears and reasons for staying were valid and real. Upheaving the family system can traumatize children if not done properly. It's still not easy on them when it is. Staying, on the other hand, even when one wants to leave, does offer some stability at home. It also offers a model of relationship where implicit and manipulative tactics of guilt and emotional blackmail become the learned way of getting what one wants. Children are also like sponges who absorb their parents dynamic and affect. They also feel the underlying anxiety and unhappiness their parents feel. All of this gets imprinted on their internal relationship map. Sometimes, this gets felt so deeply by children, they then unconsciously begin to create crises in the family. They act out in a noble but misplaced attempt to keep the family together, because they feel their parents' unhappiness and desire to leave.

"Uncoupling work" in therapy, such as "leaving with love," "divorcing with dignity," and "conscious uncoupling," can beautifully model for children that endings are a part of life. This is not always easy, though, especially if one is involved with a manipulative partner. Most likely, they won't agree to letting the other go, as they can't tolerate the loss. Unfortunately, "pick your poison" becomes the choice on the table.

Even if one is not involved with a manipulative partner, leaving needs to be done thoughtfully and with the assistance of a seasoned therapist, who can help hold the couple through the transition.

Gender Differences for Men in Divorce

The loss of self applies to men too, when their partner wants to leave. If they are still in love with their wife, then the devastation is just as deep. When men see their wives as extensions of themselves, however, rather than a separate individual with her own wants and needs, this loss turns into a huge narcissistic injury. Their world and identity, which are wrapped up with their spouse and the network of family and friends, comes crumbling down. Some men become violent (though most don't), as they can't tolerate the rage that protects the parts of them that now feel alone, helpless, and abandoned.

Understanding the History of Leaving

People will leave, in spite of public outcry and the social and familial wars that might be waged. I believe Helen would still leave Menelaus for Paris because in the land of Argos (ancient Greece), women, regardless of beauty, were still considered second-class citizens. She was young and fell in love with another. Some believe the Trojan War had little to do with Helen, as for many years, King Agamemnon of Greece had been looking for a reason to invade Troy. The cuckolding of his brother gave him one. Isn't it ironic that Helen became the "home-/country-wrecker" and her husband and brother-in-law Spartan heroes?

The friends and countrymen of the Roman empire also war-mongered. They loved Marc Antony when he remained loyal to them, but when he had ideas that differed from that of Rome's, they didn't take it too well as the narcissistic alliance was broken. Yes, Marc Antony was ambitious; some feared that like Julius Caesar, Marc Antony's alliance with Cleopatra would give him more power than they were comfortable with. They too took advantage of his love for a woman to justify their actions and ulterior motives.

Shakespeare and other authors have interpreted Plutarch's account of Antony and Cleopatra as both an epic and tragic love story. Some historians believe the lovers' motives were rooted in ambition. It's fair to say that both are true. They were star-crossed lovers who found the other to be a complementary and equal match, sharing a vision of a life together as both rulers and lovers.

Marc Antony spent many years torn between his love for Rome, which included a high military status as part of the Triumvirate, and his love for Cleopatra. The latter came with power and status but also included the added bonus of the alluring and sensuous culture of Egypt, which opened up his soul. A striking contrast to his life and wife(s) in Rome, Cleopatra showed Mark Antony a whole new world. Their affair went on for many years. Yet the ideals and values of matriarchal Egypt greatly threatened those of patriarchal Rome. Afraid of losing the love of his homeland, he proved his loyalty to Rome after his first wife died by marrying Octavius Caesar's sister, a choice that devastated Cleopatra.

As time went by, though, he longed for what he had lost. After setting sail for Egypt, Marc Antony never set foot on Roman soil again. A sort of ancient version of *Thelma and Louise*, when Antony's army deserted him, and Octavius Caesar captured Cleopatra, this couple refused to be dishonored the way the Romans would have liked. Just as they risked everything in their lives to be together, they chose to die free as well. Though their story is called a tragedy, one could argue the real tragedy would have been if Antony stayed in Rome.

The Secret to Lasting Love

When I talk to couples who have been happy together for twenty, thirty, and forty-plus years, I often ask them the following question: If you partner wanted to leave you, what would that be like for you? They all respond basically the same way, saying they would be very sad and that it would be hard to imagine life without the other. But many of them said this: "I would let them leave because I would want them to be happy." They intuitively practice the magic formula that Stephen Mitchell wrote about: love needs connection, and desire needs freedom. This is why their love lasts. They make time for each other, do fun things together, allow themselves to be vulnerable, and they listen to and hear each other's concerns. They also give each other space and have their own identity that's differentiated from their partner. They are able to reinvent themselves as they grow and change through time. They respect their partner's autonomy and know firsthand that "if you love someone, set them free, and if they come back to you, then it was meant to be." This creates the sense of freedom that desire needs.

There is nothing easy about setting someone free if they ask to leave. It takes great courage to do so, and there is grief involved. It is the right thing to do, though, if one's partner really wants to go. Psychologist James Lynch shares a heartbreaking story of one of his patients who had the revelation of the consequences of staying with a man she knew deep down didn't love her. Her insight came after she was diagnosed with potentially fatal non-Hodgkin's lymphoma. Trying to speak while weeping, these words came out of her mouth: "How could I have wasted so many years of my life? What was I thinking? I must have had a hole in my head to live with a man who did not love me."[xxvi]

Therapy helps people grieve this kind of loss and stay dignified for the sake of their children. It takes time to move through the pain. Once they do get to the other side, they often say how grateful they are they let the other go. Being held in therapy through all the messy stages of grief (which will be discussed more in part 3) allowed them to grow, heal, transform, and ultimately find a partner who wanted to stay with them through thick and thin. While at first they desperately hoped their partner would change their mind and come back, they later acknowledge how they wouldn't even consider going back if that option were available. They took responsibility for themselves and grieved.

There's a well-known saying: "Time heals all wounds," but I am not convinced it's true. I have seen people harbor their pain, anger, and anguish for twenty-plus years and more because they didn't know how to grieve the loss. With that in mind, I believe people heal all their wounds, and it takes time.

A final thought on leaving: one of my dearest of friends, also a therapist, almost left her twenty-year marriage for someone else. She tells me all the time how glad she is she stayed with her husband and that their marriage is the best it's ever been. On the flip side, I also have friends and clients who tried to leave their marriages that they had long outgrown and then balked on their decision. They chose to stay, in part because staying was easier and more comfortable but also because either their therapists, partners, or family convinced them that staying was the right thing to do, even when their hearts said otherwise. Years later, they shared their regrets. Choosing to leave is never an easy decision. And while it takes great courage to stay and try to reinvent the relationship, it also takes courage to follow one's inner truth, risk disappointing others, and leave.

In my work, I often challenge the cultural convictions of marriage that cling to the fairy tale of a love story where everyone lives happily ever after. This clinging causes pain and turns the troubled couple into a dysfunctional package that feels as though it's wrapped in a sentimental bow. Learning to embrace disillusionment empowers people. It gives them the courage to speak their truth and live their truth. It invites asking and risking rejection rather than manipulating and destroying desire. When this way of being happens with couples in therapy, they can then either learn how to end their partnership with love or discover a whole new world of possibility between them, should they stay together. Either way, an honest and authentic choice gets to be made.

Feature Story: Dysfunction Wrapped in a Sentimental Bow

Don't fear the reaper. You'll be able to fly.
—Blue Oyster Cult

For a few years, there was a story circulating on Facebook. I believe it was written anonymously. Nonetheless, the headline reads something like: "He told her he was leaving, and she asked him for just one thing." The story goes on to say something like this: Mary and John have been married for twenty years. They have a fifteen-year-old son. John fell in love with another woman and asked Mary for a divorce. Mary said she would grant that wish provided he did one thing: for the next thirty days, she wanted him to carry her down the stairs and through the door, like he did when they were first married. John agreed. The first few days of this exercise felt awkward to him. He began to notice that she had lost some weight and seemed frail. By the fourth week, the feelings of love he once had for his wife came back to him, and he told his lover that he still loved his wife and no longer wanted a divorce. He then ran back home, only to find Mary dead in their bed. Unbeknownst to him, she was dying of cancer. Mary kept her terminal illness a secret to protect her family from the pain of knowing she was dying and save her son from the scar of a divorce.

After Mary died, John wept with regret, and everyone else wept for her loss.

There's a lot that can be said about this story. It is a bit of a tearjerker upon first read. Yet let's try to answer the following question before we break out the Kleenex: Is the author of this story trying to recapture the fairy tale Mary once had with her husband twentysome years ago or expressing a sentimentally gift-wrapped revenge fantasy because John chose to leave? For argument's sake and good dialectics, let's say it's both and start with the fairy tale.

Fairy tales and myths predominate our culture and with good reason. They are both poignant and fun. Little Red Riding Hood, Cinderella, Snow White and the Seven Dwarfs, and Santa Clause fill our imaginations with adventure, hope, fear, and love, and in some cases, they can offer us guidance on how to live our lives. The story of Santa Claus may be perhaps one of the best fables for couples who want to understand the secret for a successful relationship. Why might that be, you ask? Parents who are attuned to their children's needs delight in surprising them with gifts.

Couples who are attuned with each other delight in doing the same. And though not everyone celebrates Christmas, the theme is universal. Healthy, happy couples choose to make the fairy tale real once the honeymoon phase ends. They see the inevitable misattunements, when they let each other down, as an opportunity to get curious about what happened and grow deeper their connection. This is how they make Santa real, time and time again. This is how they create and recreate the magic, even when the demands of work, family, and life take over. Though there's never a 100 percent guarantee that making it and keeping it real will last till death do us part, it is the best strategy for getting there, if that's what both parties want and continue to want.

What I most wonder about in the story of Mary and John is their capacity to reinvent themselves after the fairy tale ended. Were they able to walk down the stairs hand in hand and through the door together as equals and carry each other at different times when needed? The author doesn't say. As a psychotherapist, I am going to say probably not, and they are not alone in that matter. What we do know from the story is that he found someone else, and she is dying and doesn't tell him. We also know that she wants to relive some elements of the fairy tale with him before she passes. Who could blame her? Yet the specific tactics the author endows Mary with to help her get what she wants disempowers her. I can't help but wonder if those same tactics took place in the marriage, reflecting part of the reason their marriage fell apart.

The first tactic is guilt. Guilt is a powerful motivator, one that can never be underestimated. She guilts John into carrying her down the stairs each day because he's leaving her. He did love her once and probably feels bad for hurting her by asking her for a divorce.

The second tactic is secrecy. Perhaps there was something noble about keeping her illness a secret to protect her family from the pain of her impending death and save her son from the scar of a divorce. On the flip side, this choice was really rather cruel. Most families would want to know this so they could prepare for the loss. It is also arguable that Mary had darker motives, choosing to seduce John through guilt and manipulation, only to then abandon him with her death. The proverb "Revenge is a dish best served cold" might be applicable here.

Wouldn't it have been nice if the author endowed both Mary and John with courage? We could change the ending to have Mary say the following when John tells her he wants to leave: "John, I know we lost our way, and I don't really know why. I do know that we are both responsible for it and that we never talked about our growing distance. I regret that, and I hope you do too. I am dying. What I would really like from you is to be here for me during my final days. Do you think you could do that for me?"

Feel the difference?

This would allow them to end their marriage with love. And while I can appreciate that many would like to change the story entirely to have Mary and John stay together and work things out, that's a different story.

Endings are sad. But they are not always bad. The longing and ache we feel in our souls to live an authentic life is just as powerful a motivator as guilt, though guilt can actually feel more authentic to some. In my clinical practice, I often see people who are polarized between the two. "Should I stay or should I go?" becomes the focus in therapy until this polarization dissolves. If one has the bravery and will to get to the heart of the matter, then it will.

There's a line from the Semisonic song "Closing Time" that says, "Every new beginning starts from some other beginning's end." Yet I prefer Blue Oyster Cult to close out this story, to honor both the phenomena of endings and the gift of disillusionment:

"Don't fear the reaper. You'll be able to fly."

Color Commentary

While this feature story shows the woman as the one utilizing manipulative tactics to keep the other and the man as having abandoned his wife without really trying to fix things first, it's worth stating the obvious here: both sexes in heterosexual and same-sex marriages engage in this kind of behavior, to avoid the pain of feeling abandoned or feeling lonely.

CHAPTER 6

Befindlichkeit: When Love's Labor Really Is Lost

> We do not say: Being is, time is, but rather:
> there is Being and there is Time.
> —Martin Heidegger

German philosopher Martin Heidegger used the word *befindlichkeit* to mean "being in a mood." His book *Being in Time* has become an existential bible for many who desperately try to find hope in their crisis. When they come to see me for therapy, I use a crasser and more visceral translation of that word to help them make sense of their circumstances. Before I share my translation, let me first paint a picture of what that moment before they make the call to ask for help looked like for them and what it may look like for you.

It's common these days for many people to find themselves feeling hopelessly trapped in a terrible tempest when their love's labor's lost. Whether they are starting over again after a divorce or the death of their loved one, entangled in the web of infidelity (either their partner's, their own, or being the other in the triangle), hoodwinked by manipulation and abuse, or discovering that they are the one hoodwinking, longing to leave a partner or fighting to make their partner stay, not realizing that they don't have a strong survival strategy, they do realize that if they don't take some kind of action, they will succumb to the storm. Refusing to do that, they take the advice given in the last chapter before they are really ready to. They put on some Blue Oyster Cult and will themselves to not fear the reaper. And just as they take that leap of faith, feeling euphoric and believing they will land in greener pastures, they discover their plane has no fuel and they are about to crash into a big pile of shit.

Feeling lost, angry and hopeless as they begin to make their way out of the manure, they conclude that they don't fear the reaper, they just think he's a fraud. Felling a tad jaded but not wanting to be bitter, they clean themselves up, make a martini with lots of olives, put on some Leonard Cohen, and hope that when David plays his "secret chord" they will have a "hallelujah" moment, as they stand by and wait for some hope.

It doesn't come.

They find themselves in befindlichkeit, or as I like to say to my clients when they first walk through my office door, "Congratulations, you are in the shit."

"Being in the shit" is an expression that clowns use as they master their comedic craft. As comedians and clowns know all too well, once fully emerged in it, creative possibilities arise because they know how to play with pain. So do therapists, but in a different way. When people find themselves in a crisis of love's labor's lost, feeling like they are damned if they do and damned if 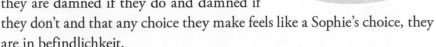 they don't and that any choice they make feels like a Sophie's choice, they are in befindlichkeit.

If they come to therapy, they learn that their suffering grew out of two deeply polarized parts of them that had radically different ideas on how to solve the problem they were struggling with. These parts were just trying to protect something more vulnerable deep inside the recess of their souls; people soon discover that these parts were just looking in the wrong direction, outside rather than in.

Never did I know that a frog trapped in a sewer croaked a metaphorical message for me, one that answered the question on how to help my clients choose to make that U-turn[6] and discover hope along the path

---

[6] "U-Turn" is a phrase from couples therapist Toni Herbin-Blank

of psychotherapy. I owe this message to a client. After she rekindled an affair she had ended so she could work on her marriage, as her friends, family, and previous therapist encouraged her to do, she found herself in a pit of despair. Finding herself torn between trying to do what everyone, including part of herself, thought was the right thing to do and what her heart and soul really wanted to do, she told me about a loud frog in her backyard that kept her up one night. Stopping to listen to it helped her quiet her mind and gave her a sense of peace. Ironically, at that same time, there was a frog that was croaking loudly in a sewer outside my home, which gave my neighbors and me angst. My experience in dealing with my own angst triggered by the frog reminded me that no matter what crisis you find yourself in, there's always hope.

Feature Story: A Frog Trapped in a Sewer

Free yourself to be yourself.
—U2, "Iris"

Ahimsa means nonviolence.

In Vedic and Buddhist philosophies, there's a belief in the equality of all sentient beings. The practice of ahimsa, which can also be thought of as compassion and self-compassion, extends toward all of them.

Last month, there was a frog that appeared to be trapped in a sewer on my street. Night after night, for the entire month, I would hear it croak loudly from my home office window. As I would walk my dogs by it, the frog seemed to croak even louder, almost as if were pleading for help to escape. I spoke to several neighbors to get their thoughts on the frog, and they too worried that it might be stuck in there with no way out. I found myself wondering if there was anything I could do to set it free, and it pained me to know that there wasn't.

As a psychotherapist, I work with many people who feel utterly trapped in their current life circumstances, like the frog. They see no immediate way out and often begin to feel resigned to being stuck in their own personal sewer. Being stuck feels lousy. Getting unstuck feels scary, sometimes even terrifying. More often than not, many prefer feeling the dysthymic sense of stuckness over the terrifying possibility of becoming free. They then waffle between the two polarities, sometimes for a very long time. This waffling, however, is a necessary part of the process should one truly desire the risk, reward, and responsibility of becoming a free and individuated self.

One night, after a month of listening to the frog and my own agonizing feelings that I was projecting onto it (who knows? It may have been enjoying its time down there), I walked over to the sewer where it lived. I spent some time sending compassionate energy toward it and waited until its croaks and my angst quieted. Then I walked back into the house, knowing there was nothing more I could do.

The next night, I didn't hear the frog. I walked the dogs a couple of times by the sewer to check on it. I feared it may have died. Then, as I walked the dogs back home and entered my garage, I saw something move out of the corner of my eye. Lo and behold, it was a frog hopping its way through an obstacle course of randomly stored and overstacked stuff.

Seeing it gave me such joy, as I imagined the frog found the courage to free itself so that it could be itself.

Six weeks passed since I terminated therapy with the frog (kidding), but what a case study it was. It reminded me of the power of possibility when we practice and surrender to ahimsa, compassion, and compassion with ourselves and others.

It also made me wonder what would happen if we all dared ask the question, what if?

Color Commentary: What If?

Carl Jung said, "When people look outside themselves, they dream. When they look inside themselves, they awaken." What if traditional talk psychotherapy began integrating inside somatic work that embraces the concepts of ahimsa and self-compassion, to help heal the implicit memories of one's internal relationship map? What if there was a way to access the language of those memories and hear the story it wants to tell but only does so through sensation?

Traditional talk therapy offers clients a compassionate relationship where they can come to understand who they are and why they act out what they do with their partners; through the therapeutic relationship itself, they learn how to relate differently with others in the world. It does not, however, help clients access the implicit memories of their relationship maps.

What if therapy could foster both the relationship you get in talk therapy and the mind/body techniques that could help you heal your inner attachment and recalibrate your internal compass and relationship map?

What if therapy opened the door to an inner resource inside of you that allowed you to feel calm, compassionate, and curious about your crises, that you could access at any time?

What if, suddenly and unexpectedly, you discovered something utterly profound about yourself, and through that discovery, some kind of creative insight and solution to your crises came to you, like a flash of inspiration?

What if you found hope?

PART 2

Finding Hope: The Road Back Home

CHAPTER 7

Who Put Hope in the Box?
Why Hope Always Springs Eternal

I'm something from nothing.
—Dave Grohl

A long time ago, before the construct of time even existed, the mystery of dark nothingness loomed. What happened next has been imagined many times, many ways, in many different cultures, by many a seeker, who longed to understand how all of creation came into being. This next event was that somehow, someway, something came out of nothing. The Greek and Roman poets Hesiod and Ovid were just two of the many who imagined this something from nothing metamorphosis. Ovid called this something "Chaos" and described it as "primordial, …[where] land and sea and air existed… [and] all matter remained formless, shapeless, forever changing and at war within."[xxvii] He imagined and hypothesized that after Chaos came Gaia, perhaps even through Chaos itself, who was the mother earth and served as both the earth itself and its creation goddess. She became the yin to Chaos's (who was sexless) yang. Driven by the energetic force of Eros (who later became the Greek god of sexual attraction), the two mated. Through their union, Chao's formless matter shape-shifted and created the universe. As Gaia and Chaos continued mating, Uranus, the sky, appeared next. Totally captivated by Gaia, Uranus wrapped himself around her, just as the sky wraps around the earth, and created a sphere where life on Gaia's land also shape-shifted and came to be. As Gaia's consort, the two then created twelve children, called Titans: six female and six male; the youngest was a boy named Cronos. Uranus did not like his children, perhaps because Gaia's attention went to them rather than him, so he shoved them all back into Gaia's womb. Both frustrated with Uranus's behavior and tired of the discomfort of having twelve children in her belly, Gaia developed a plan, which Cronos helped execute. When Uranus returned to mate with Gaia, Cronos castrated his father. Uranus then left Gaia alone, and their children got to be born again.

Cronos then became his sister Rhea's consort, and the two had six children, three girls and three boys, one of whom was named Zeus. But as they say, like father, like son. Cronos did not like his children either, and the legacy repeated when Zeus destroyed Cronos and the other Titans with his very own lightning bolt. He and his siblings then settled down on Mount Olympus.

One second-generation Titan, named Prometheus, was too busy creating the human race to get taken out by Zeus. Sculpted from Gaia's silty clay, this race consisted only of men. None too happy with Zeus, Prometheus tried to get one over on him when he rationed off portions of meat from a sacred bull, meant to be evenly divided between the gods and man. Instead of a fair division of meat, he took the bull's bones and covered it with fat to make it seem more appealing to Zeus and placed it next to a seemingly ordinary cut of meat, waiting for Zeus to choose. Seeing through this trick, Zeus chose the bones, allowing Prometheus to think he won. Little did Prometheus know that at that moment, Zeus had the upper hand. Zeus denied humans the gift of fire and forced them to eat their meat raw. Unhappy with being duped, Prometheus then stole the fire from Mount Olympus and gave it to man. That was the last straw for Zeus, though, and he began plotting his ultimate revenge, one which would affect the human race forever.

Just as Prometheus created men from clay, Zeus gathered Gaia's adobe and sculpted the first woman, who he named Pandora. Pandora, which means "all gifts," was meant to be a gift to men and a peace offering to Prometheus, from the king of the gods himself. Adding a woman to the human clan would allow the race a chance of survival. While creating Pandora, Zeus got his siblings, the other gods and goddesses, to endow her with beauty, grace, and charm, as well as the gifts of ravenous lust, treachery, and shamelessness.[xxviii]

When Pandora descended from Mount Olympus, she carried with her a beautiful box. This box contained Zeus's revenge, as inside the chest were sickness, old age, wickedness, immorality, and other vices waiting patiently to be released. Pandora didn't know what was in the chest and became curious; she opened it herself, and what flew out of the chest took her by surprise. Once she understood the gravity of what was happening, as these vices were meant to give men the experience of pain and suffering, she quickly closed the box. The only thing left in it was hope.

While the story of Pandora has traditionally implied that women are both gifts to the world as well the cause of the world's suffering, there's another and perhaps more important way to understand this myth, one that we need to figure out for ourselves to really get it. It starts with asking, who put hope in the box, and why did they do that? I don't know the answer, but I do know that both the box and Pandora are made from the element, earth, which is Gaia herself, and that hope is inside of it.

What if Gaia got tired of witnessing the legacy of men waging war against each other, reenacting their father-son rivalry, and wanted peace? What if she saw through Zeus's insulting plot, which involved using Pandora as his scapegoat and blaming her for his actions? What if she purposefully placed hope in that box, knowing that it would be the last item in it and that her wisdom, which lived in the grains of clay that Pandora was made of, would intuitively tell Pandora to shut the box before hope got out? Perhaps this gift of hope remained inside the box, not outside it, to serve as an important clue on how we as human beings could honestly and authentically access it?

It's reasonable to assume that we have been misinterpreting the real meaning of hope all these years, just has we have been misinterpreting the real meaning of the myth of Pandora, which implicates women being the gift bearers of human pain and suffering.

Hope has traditionally been defined as "a feeling or expectation for a certain thing to happen." Through this lens, hope is a setup, especially when it comes to healing the crises of love's labor's lost. It's a setup because it requires external factors to happen, something outside of ourselves, which we have no real control over, in order to relieve our suffering and make us happy.

Perhaps Gaia knew, just as all good therapists know, the secret for allowing authentic change starts when people experience the struggle with all things considered, not just the crises of love's labor's lost. What if an important step in revealing that secret was that people have to have their own process of discovery and their own findings, not the findings of others, to authentically heal and change? What if this process was actually an inward journey, perhaps even an odyssey, that takes time, ranging from two years to two millennia?

It doesn't matter whether Gaia herself actually gave humankind a gift of genuine hope by putting it in the box or not. Hope is inside of it, not outside of it, just as hope is inside of you, not outside of you. Anyone can find hope because it's an energetic force; different cultures have different names for it, and it eternally lives inside every human's heart. I believe that people are just looking for it in the wrong direction; the first thing they need to do is to turn around and come home to themselves. That's the key people need to open the door to discover who they are and become who they are meant to be. When they use that key, they will find the hope inside of them, the energetic force and key to shape-shifting any crisis in love's labor's lost.

Feature Story: Seven Simple Ways to Shape-Shift Your Life When You're Feeling Down for the Count

> Nothing is impossible. The word itself says I'm possible.
> —Audrey Hepburn

Albert Einstein shamelessly stated, "Imagination is more important than knowledge." A renegade physicist most known for his equation $E = MC^2$, Einstein believed that energy could not be created or destroyed, just changed from one form to another. His ideas spoke to the heart of the culturally diverse and timeless fascination of shape-shifting.

Shape-shifting is "the ability of a being or creature to completely transform its physical form or shape." This common theme in ancient mythology and shamanism involves a magical transformation from one state to another, often from human to animal. In the modern era, shape-shifting has become a widely used metaphor for variety of genres.

Sports is one such genre. Those who live in New England or follow its teams will remember the Boston Bruins 2011 playoffs. Fans rode the roller coaster of constant come-from-behind wins (accompanied by Jack Edwards's historic commentary) from the quarterfinals in Montreal all the way to claiming Lord Stanley's Cup in Vancouver. The B's shape-shifted again and again until they emerged victorious. Then there was Malcolm Butler's against-all-odds (and -ergonomics) game-winning interception in Super Bowl XLIX. With twenty-six seconds left in the game and

Marshawn Lynch inches from the end zone, Seattle Seahawk players and fans began celebrating the seemingly inevitable game-winning touchdown. The Patriots then shape-shifted and dashed the Seahawks' hopes. In 2017, they did it again. Down 28–3 in the third, the Falcons smelled victory. Tom Brady marched down the field and showed the world once again that miracles do happen (sometimes). What seemed fated to be an epic loss shape-shifted into one of the most legendary Super Bowl victories to date.

Shape-shifting happens in psychotherapy too, though in this genre, most keep bragging rights to themselves. People come to therapy when they feel down for the count and desperately seek to transform their lives. While therapy may not be for everyone, almost everyone has found themselves at some point in dire need of change. If you can relate to that sentiment, then here are seven simple shape-shifting techniques you can practice on your own to begin turning your life around.

1. *Ask yourself the following question: If anything were possible and nothing mattered, what does my heart long to be, do, or have?* The sky's the limit, so be brave. Right now, this secret desire gets to live privately and safely within the walls of your imagination. No one has to know about it, except you. Feel what happens in your body when you do this. Compare that in-the-body feeling with your feelings toward your current situation (or whatever it is you think you should be, do, or have). Notice the contrast. Without thinking, kinesthetically feel which thought or idea makes your heart lift.

2. *Focus on what does lift your heart,* imagining yourself being, doing, or having it. Sense and feel what happens in your body.

3. *Allow the parts of you that tell you why you can't (or shouldn't) be, do, or have this to come forward.* Sense and feel them in your body.

4. *Send all those naysayer parts of you lots of compassion.* Contrary to what many people say, pushing aside or ignoring fears doesn't work. Those parts of you have important messages and concerns that want and need to be heard. They have good intentions and are trying to protect you from deeper held beliefs and fears in your inner system. Listen to all their concerns, and then channel Aaron Rodgers's invitation for relaxation toward them all.

5. *Allow the deeper fears to emerge in their own time and way.* (If this becomes overwhelming, then you may want to consider psychotherapy.) Listen with compassion to all your pain—every last drop of it—and allow it to dissipate.

6. *Shift your focus* back again to what makes your heart happy and feel what happens again in your body.

7. *Wait and listen.* Allow yourself to be guided by your heart's intuition and follow its lead by taking whatever inspired actions it asks of you.

Practice this simple technique three minutes a day, three times a day for three weeks, three months, or three years, and watch your life begin to transform. You can shape-shift anything in your life, if it's what your heart truly desires. If it's not, then it won't happen, no matter how hard you try. Trust that your heart has an inner wisdom in wanting what it wants, whatever that may be.

While Shakespeare's Hamlet tormented over "whether tis nobler to suffer the slings and arrows of outrageous fortune," and many have followed in suit, I believe there's a better way. What lifts your heart, at least the essences of it, is what you are supposed to be, do, or have. When you surrender to that and set your intention to allow for what you really want to flow into your life, you will discover some really good news. What makes you happy, when pursued in a kind, compassionate, and loving way, is always in the best interest of the greater good.

Why not give it a try and see what happens?

You never know what dreams may come.

Color Commentary

Hope has become a heroine with a thousand faces, throughout time, crisis, and situation. In the Vedic/Hindu tradition, hope the way I am describing it in this chapter is called Atman, which means self or soul. In the Judeo-Christian tradition, hope can be considered God or Christ's love. In both the East and West, the energetic force of hope, regardless of what name it's given, lives from a metaphysical perspective both inside and outside the human heart. You don't have to subscribe to any particular faith, or any faith at all, however, to access it. If you simply see it as tapping into an inner state of curious, calm, creative energy[xxix] that everyone has within, this energy can rewire the stress response to your crisis. It's why meditation, yoga, and tai chi have become so popular.

In psychotherapy, there's a methodology that helps people access hope and use it to heal their inner attachments and relationship maps to begin making their way out of the crisis of love's labor's lost. It's the first step in finding the creative solution to their polarizing problem.

CHAPTER 8

Self-Energy: How to Turn that Frown Upside Down

Hope is the thing with feathers that perches in the soul.
—Emily Dickinson

Couples therapist Toni Herbine-Blank teaches people to heal their attachment style (relationship map), which lends to the crisis of love's labor's lost, by integrating the psychodynamic framework shared in part 1 with a newer model of psychotherapy that offers hope. In therapy, the therapist creates a good enough holding environment (like parents and caretakers, therapists make mistakes too), one in which a client can begin to develop a true self; see chapter 2 for more on this. Since the implicit memories that create the insecure attachment style stored in one's relationship map are often stored in the body or places in the brain that language has a hard time accessing,[xxx] talk therapy doesn't always help people fully access and heal the trauma that created those maps in the first place. Healing this trauma helps people recalibrate their relationship maps, so that they can find authentic and creative solutions to their crises.

Richard Schwartz, originally a family systems therapist, developed a model that helps people access those places, or what he calls "parts" of themselves, in a loving and compassionate way. He named this model the Internal Family Systems Model of Psychotherapy,[xxxi] as it uses hope (which he calls "Self-energy") to do the job. He describes Self-energy as an inner state of calm, creative, clear, curious, compassionate energy that makes taking the journey inside of oneself a lot less daunting.

In Herbine-Blank's book, *Intimacy from the Inside Out: Courage and Compassion in Couple Therapy,* she illustrates how an integration of both models can be highly effective, making it safe for people and couples to do what she calls a U-turn[xxxii] in therapy. Instead of looking outside themselves either to their partners or others to take care of their pain, they learn to turn around and look within. This helps people get off the seesaw and roller coaster of hope and hopelessness that couples who first come to therapy find themselves stuck on: Feeling hopeful and up when they believe the other will do this drops to a sense hopeless and helpless when the other doesn't. For example, Alyssa had been dating Terrence for five years. She loved him and wanted to marry him, but his excessive and even obsessive need to clean and organize (and criticize her when she wasn't) often sent her into a rage. She wanted him to be more go with the flow and less anal, just as she was. She asked Terrance to be a little more lax, which he in earnest would try to do for her and could succeed for short periods of time.

When he inevitably would return to the behavioral style that he knew, Alyssa would get upset. She made her happiness contingent upon his actions. Through therapy, she was able to start to understand why she got so upset in the first place, when she found enough Self-energy to take her first U-turn.

Take a moment to think of something you may be struggling with in your life. Now ask yourself this question: "What if I had an inner resource inside of me that will keep me calm, curious, and compassionate, no matter what happens?" While that may seem impossible, it's not. What if hope and Self-energy were energetic states, like the relaxation response or the Taoist concept of flow, which resides in the treasure chest of the human heart?

When you connect to your own Self-energy, you have now found hope in your crisis. It will allow you to surrender to what is, even when that is not what you want, so you can create space and possibility for what actually can be. Here's an example of how going inside and connecting to Self-energy can help:

Clinical Case of Stacey

Stacey came to see me because she was having an affair. She wanted to leave her husband and be with her lover. She thought that therapy would be just one or two sessions, as her mind was pretty much made up; she made it clear that she was doing this to placate her husband and family, who did not want her to leave. Other therapists told her that what she was doing was wrong and that she should give up her lover and honor her marriage vows, which at that time she did not want to do.

She looked quite shocked and seemed relieved when I said (my usual), "I don't know what the right decision is for you. Sometimes people stay in their marriages and work things out. Other times, they follow their hearts and deal with the guilt. What is right for you is ultimately your call. I just think that before you finalize your decision, you may want to look deeper inside of yourself and heal whatever needs to be healed first. This way, you will make an authentic choice, and as a clinician, that is the only thing I really care about."

That message spoke to her, which in turn created a therapeutic contract, which is a piece of work the therapist and client agree to focus on in the therapy. Stacey genuinely wanted to make an authentic choice about whether she should stay in her marriage or not. I suggested that the only way she could make that choice was by taking a U-turn and looking inside to understand what was driving this crisis of love's labor's lost (though I didn't use that phrase).

On her way out the door after her first appointment, Stacey turned and said, "Wow, I wasn't expecting this to happen," as she expected me to say to her what others had, which was that what she was doing was bad and wrong. My curiosity and compassion for her crisis sparked her own, and she had a little taste of what Self-energy was.

This taste deepened during her second appointment when she revealed her agony, as she shared an unpleasant interaction with her husband earlier that day. While telling me about it, Stacey became increasingly distressed. I asked her to pause and to notice what she was experiencing in her body. She complained that she felt a lot of tension in the back of her neck and could feel a headache coming on. Her chest felt tight, and her heart was racing. I asked her to close her eyes, take some deep breaths, and focus on the sensations she was experiencing before she continue on with the story. As she did this, her demeanor quieted. When I asked her what she was noticing, she said she felt more relaxed and that her headache and neck tension were softening, as was the tightness in her chest. I encouraged her to continue sending this newly found calm energy to the tense areas to see if it could release even more. It did. She found her Self-energy, her hope in the crisis again.

Stacey opened her eyes and remained calm as she told me the rest of the story. Though we didn't delve much deeper into anything else in this session, as moving too quickly into the work can be overwhelming for those new to therapy, helping her connect to her Self-energy and take a U-turn back to herself gave her relief from her somatic symptoms. Though nothing had externally changed in her life during this appointment, something internally did. She now had the hope she needed to find her authentic and creative solution to her crisis and trusted that in time, she would know what that creative solution would be. After a four-year course of psychotherapy, she found it indeed.

Stacey came to therapy when she was experiencing enough discomfort in her life that made her want to do something about it. People generally don't come to therapy or seek to make any changes in their life until they get uncomfortable. We ungodly therapists have our own discomfort, just as mere mortals do. When Stacey came to see me, I was having a parallel process with her discomfort, as it triggered some of my own discomfort in a personal matter that differed from hers. So I took a rescue remedy trip to the Berkshires with a good friend and colleague, and wrote the next story for her.

Feature Story: Opening the Window

> And it goes so slowly on,
> everything I've ever wanted,
> tell me what's wrong.
> —The Replacements

Nobody likes change.

Most resist it until they can do so no longer. Only when optimal discomfort (a clinical term) takes place do people then begin to embrace what they can no longer deny: something's got to shift. It's called optimal discomfort because too much discomfort creates panic and resistance, and not enough leads to continued stuckness, a condition many are comfortable in.

This past summer, I took an annual trip to Kripalu in the Berkshires with a friend and colleague who is also a therapist. The rooms there are simple and clean. There are windows and a fan, but no air conditioning. Summer days in the Berkshires can be extremely hot and humid, and though it does cool off at night, the rooms at Kripalu tend to hold onto the heat from the day.

The first night, I tossed and turned for most of it. Around two in the morning, my friend whispered from across the room, "You can always open the window, you know. You might sleep better."

I responded, "That would require me to get up," and we both laughed. Though I was uncomfortable, I wasn't uncomfortable enough to do anything about it.

In therapy, many of my clients share their quiet discontent with me, often for a long time before they are ready to make any changes. This is part of the process, however. My job is to create a space that allows them to honestly explore their level of dissatisfaction, whether it's with work or a relationship, until they become dissatisfied enough to do something about it; hence, they experience optimal discomfort. Sometimes, therapy helps people learn to better tolerate conditions that they aren't ready to do anything about, and sometimes, it empowers them to be bold and take the risk their heart and soul desires. Either way, nothing changes on the outside, until something changes on the inside first.

The second night at Kripalu, I began to toss and turn again while trying to sleep. Though the temperature during the day and night were roughly the same as the previous day, something inside of me wanted something different: to sleep better. So around two o'clock, I quietly tiptoed out of bed to open up the window.

I wasn't quiet enough, however, as I heard a voice from across the room ask, "What are you doing?"

"Opening the window," I whispered back, and then we both burst out laughing.

Optimal discomfort allowed me to create space for something new, which in this case was more fresh air and a soft breeze that led to good night's sleep.

Imagine what optimal discomfort might allow you to create space for in your life.

Color Commentary

Optimal discomfort, Self-energy, and U-turns are the first steps to be taken in psychotherapy; they help people find the hope in their crisis of love's labor's lost. The journey to finding authentic creative solutions gets even more fascinating when people then start to look and travel even deeper inside of themselves.

CHAPTER 9

Pop Goes the Weasel: Befriending What's Inside the Jack in the Box

If you gaze long enough into the abyss, the abyss will gaze back at you.
—Friedrich Nietzsche

Once people get enough of an experience of their own Self-energy, they soon become curious enough to start to look inside of themselves. Still somewhat afraid that they might be looking into an empty abyss or, even worse, that they'll hear the creepy melody of the jack in the box song and some weasel will pop up and scare them, that fear soon gets relieved. With Self-energy, they begin to discover some things that take them by surprise, but in a good way. They discover that they are not empty or scary at all. They have different parts of themselves that want different things, and they are so excited to be finally noticed. Once this happens, many soon ask, what the heck are parts?

The human psyche, by design, holds multiple ideas, beliefs, thoughts, and defenses that at times fiercely contradict each other. When there is developmental trauma that manifests as an insecure or disorganized attachment, parts are born.

In the Internal Family Systems (IFS) model of psychotherapy, these parts fall into two categories: protectors and exiles. When there is neglect or abuse during childhood, the burdens of fright, rage, shame, loneliness, and more can overwhelm a child. These feelings get compartmentalized and exiled in the inner system. They become the implicit memories from which an insecure attachment style develops. Richard Schwartz calls these parts "exiles." In order to keep the burdens of exiled parts at bay, other parts start to develop and protect the exiles: Protectors. They become the keeper of the gate. Their job is to protect the system from the pain and burdens of the exiles. Some protectors take on extreme roles, such as panic, depression, addiction, violence, compulsive behaviors, and dissociation, which Schwartz calls firefighters. Other protectors protect in a more socially acceptable fashion (e.g., hyperorganized, caretaking, or rescuing parts), which Schwartz calls managers. The protectors, firefighters, and managers intend solely to protect the only way they know how: by doing what they do. Remember Alyssa from the last chapter? Her husband's hyperorganized and sometimes critical behavior that would sometimes send her into a rage? She discovered what his part (i.e., the organizing and critical manager) triggered in her. When she connected with her Self-energy and somatically explored the rage, by focusing and feeling the sensation in her body, the rage gave way to her exiles: shame and sadness. As a creative child who liked to daydream and perhaps had a touch of ADD, she found that she felt happiest when she could be messy, meaning not perfect. As she explored herself in psychotherapy, she began to have memories of her father, who was very type A. He had little tolerance for anything less than perfect or perfectly clean. He often criticized Alyssa harshly, which left her feeling both bad and sad. When her husband exhibited some of the same behaviors that her father had, it would trigger her unhealed sad and shamed exiles. Once the burdens of those parts started to come forward, her fiery protector rage would take over, and she would let her husband have it.

At first, many people find the concept of protectors and exiles hard to swallow. They often say, "This isn't a part; it is me."

I then respond, saying something like, "Of course it's you. It's a very important part of you, but it's not all of you, all the time, right?"

Many parts, such as obsessive cleaning parts (a symptom of obsessive-compulsive disorder, or OCD), do have a biological basis, and medication can help treat the symptoms or, as IFS therapists say, "not work so hard." Parts can be biologically based and have a job to protect an exile at the same time. An obsessive cleaning managerial part may be working to control a panicky firefighter, whose job is to protect a person from feeling the overwhelming grief of an exile. And yes, medication (along with

Self-energy) can help those protectors relax and reduce the pain the exiles feel.

The next hurdle people sometimes have when they connect to their own Self-energy is to have compassion for parts of themselves that they may not like. I remind them that it's a part of them that doesn't like the other part and that both those parts have protective jobs and really good intentions. Here is a case example to help clarify that:

Clinical Case of Don

Don came to see me, as he was struggling in his marriage and acknowledged that he drank too much. His wife told him that she was giving him the boot if he couldn't sober up.

His story is a common one, and it didn't take long after receiving the ultimatum from his wife for him to genuinely want to get sober. During one of our sessions, we talked about a slip he had over the weekend, as he had a couple of drinks. He began to berate himself (angry protector part), as he didn't understand why he was so weak (critical protector part).

I asked him if having a couple of drinks helped him, and with a shocked look on his face, he said, "Are you crazy? It doesn't help me; it's ruining my life" (exacerbated firefighter).

He then proceeded to list all the reasons why this is so.

I then said, "Yes, there are many negative consequences to your drinking, but it does serve a purpose. What if the part of you that drinks was actually trying to help you? Why might it be doing that?"

Don paused, became curious (Self-energy), and then said, "Oh, I had a terrible fight with my wife over the weekend, and I had so much to do. Drinking (firefighter) helped me not feel so stressed and relax a little" (positive intention).

In this example, Don tapped into a little Self-energy (curiosity) and befriended the part of him that drinks. He learned that this part wasn't bad, per se, though the aftermath of its actions were far from favorable. By befriending it, he was able to look inside, and when he did, he discovered that he had a "whole lotta parts," including the critic, angry protector, and addicted part that drank, all active inside of him.

At times, discovering these "whole lotta parts," which people encounter early on in therapy, can cause a little worry and alarm. Some people hold their breath and ask me, "Am I schizophrenic, like Sybil?" trying not to be frightened over how I might answer that question.

I then respond, saying, "No, not at all. You just have an inner traffic jam that you have discovered, and it's our job to help clear that up."

Feature Story: The Traffic Jam

> With one breath, with one flow, you will know.
> —The Police, "Synchronicity"

Swiss psychiatrist Carl Jung (1875–1961) shared a story about a patient who once had a dream about an expensive piece of jewelry, which she referred to as a golden scarab.[xxxiii] Clinically, he was trying to help her get more connected to her heart, which her rational, logical, defensive mind protected her from (with good reason, I am sure). He struggled with her for quite some time and asked for a little help from the universe, which he got on the day she talked about her dream. As he listened to what she was describing, he heard a light tapping on his window. He turned around and saw that it was a golden scarab beetle, which were widely revered in ancient Egypt. He pointed this out to his patient, who quickly made the connection between her inner world being mirrored by the outer world. This synchronistic moment, which some may see as simply a coincidence (Jung saw otherwise), reportedly worked. The therapy then began to help her.

John was a client I had been working with on and off for several years. Normally on time for session, he arrived twenty minutes late, seemingly aggravated.

"Sorry," he said as he plopped himself on my couch. "I've been stuck in traffic for over an hour."

John had been feeling frustrated with many things in his life, one of which was an overseas job that he desperately wanted and had been in the works for over a year now. His fiancée lived in Europe, across the Atlantic, and the long-distance travel to see her was wearing on them both. It seemed that each time he got close to getting an offer, something would fall through. Trying to ignore his immediate experience of frustration, he dove into reporting on all the recent developments (or lack thereof) in his life.

"Being stuck in traffic really sucks," I said, to which he paused, nodded his head, and looked at me. "Can you feel the frustration in your body?" I asked.

"Yes, but I really just want to forget about it," he responded.

"Of course you do," I said, "but why not take a moment to just acknowledge it and see what happens?"

He agreed. He closed his eyes and focused on the tension in his neck and shoulders. As he followed his breath, his frustration turned to anger and then softened to a profound sadness. He acknowledged how helpless he felt regarding his current life circumstances and wished things could change. We spent the rest of the session holding that as he grieved his sense of helplessness. By the end of the appointment, there was an alchemical shift in the room. Though the therapy in and of itself couldn't do much to change the external issues in his outer life, his inner life dramatically shifted when he discovered self-compassion.

We joked as he left that evening, hoping the traffic jam would be cleared up by now so he could have an easy ride home. "It will be what it will be," he said, smiling as he walked out the door.

Two weeks later, John arrived early for his appointment. I opened my office door to see him seated in the waiting room, grinning from ear to ear.

"Guess what happened?" he asked as he entered my office.

"You tell me," I responded as I waited to hear his news.

"I got an offer that I accepted. I will be moving to Europe and starting my new job in two months."

He had his golden scarab moment, and his inner traffic jam cleared.

Whether or not one buys into Jung's theory of synchronicity doesn't matter. Taking the time to sit compassionately with all of one's parts and unburdening the pain inside does.

Why?

Because it helps us to better manage the inevitable traffic jams we all experience and then find new routes to travel on in our lives.

Befriending and the Myth of Naga Vasuki

Befriending parts—a clinical term from the IFS model, which means to understand that all parts have good intentions—is the first necessary step in helping someone begin to clear up an inner traffic jam. Many people see befriending as a new concept. It's not. It's actually quite ancient. In Vedic mythology, there's a story about an underworld serpent that shows the benefits of befriending extreme protectors (firefighters) and the consequences for not doing so. It's called the myth of Naga Vasuki.

This myth tells the story of a war between the gods and demons to gain control over the universe. Naga Vasuki was a demon serpent who ruled Patala Loka, the underworld. The gods were in search for amrita, the nectar of mortality, but they needed help from the demons to get it.

So they made a deal to team up and get it together. Naga Vasuki wrapped his snake body around the highly spiritual Mount Mandra, and the gods used his body like a rod to churn the ocean for their search. And guess what? By teaming up together, they found it.

The gods then decided to renege on the deal, as they feared what would happen if the demons drank the amrita and became immortal. They created a distraction and threw them a wild party. The gods held their own private party, where they planned to drink the amrita all by themselves.

Naga Vasuki, however, the great strategist who helped them get the amrita, saw through this ploy. He disguised himself as a god and crashed their private party. Just as he started to drink the amrita, the sun and moon figured out who he was. They warned Lord Vishnu, the creator of the universe, who immediately threw his discus at Naga Vasuki, severing his body in two. Since he already drank the amrita, though, he was now immortal and quite angry at the sun and moon for ratting him out. The severed body of Naga Vasuki metamorphosed into what the Vedics called shadow planets, named Rahu and Ketu, the head and tail of the snake now immortalized in the cosmos. They are the north and south nodal points of the ecliptic that block the light of the sun and moon which form eclipses. In ancient times, eclipses were ominous.

Amrita is much like the hope of Pandora's box. Metaphorically speaking, it is Self-energy. It can help befriend all parts of the system, which in turn can allow the box to open even wider, allowing even more Self-energy. Denying the wisdom of your inner Naga Vasuki (protective parts) eclipses the hope and Self-energy inside of you that has a creative solution to every problem. Plus, just as in the myth, in life, your inner Naga Vasuki won't stand for it, either. That's why many relapse, continue to have affairs, engage in manipulative behaviors, or act out in destructive ways. It's how those parts of you that you deny crash your party to get their due. Why not give them some attention and see what they have to say? They may actually be quite appreciative of your attention and decide they can relax back for a bit. In IFS, we call this "unblending."

Unblending from What's inside the Jack in the Box

Three things cannot be long hidden: the sun, the moon, and the truth.
—Buddha

I share the story of Naga Vasuki to encourage people to extend curious Self-energy to all their parts, which may even help some of the most destructive firefighters (addictive or self-harming parts) not work so hard. The next step is to help people unblend from these parts so that even more Self-energy can extend toward them. Once these parts trust in the safety and security of a person's Self-energy, protectors will start to unblend, opening up a pathway to the exiled parts of the system the protectors are protecting. With consistent connection with Self-energy, the protective gatekeepers start to trust that it's safe to let down their guard. This can take some time, though.

Clinical Case of Shannon

Shannon was a thirty-five-year-old woman with a fifteen-year-old cocaine addiction (firefighter). She too struggled in her marriage, as she felt neglected by her husband, a high-powered corporate executive, who seemed to spend more time at work than with her. He had had it with her drug use and gave her an ultimatum: "Quit drugs or I'm done" (his angry manager).

She tried all kinds of therapy, and at times, she white-knuckled her cravings (managing part), but she couldn't abstain from using for long. She was polarized. She loved this drug, describing it by saying, "I feel such a rush of love when I use" (positive intention) and that nothing else compared to it. She also acknowledged that it was hurting her marriage (insightful manager) and her pocketbook, as she was blowing her retirement money (overspending, compulsive firefighter) on it.

Wanting to save her marriage and possibly have children someday, Shannon had many reasons to stop. Yet she had just as many reasons to continue, as the so-called bad reasons outweighed the so-called good in her intrapersonal decisional balance sheet.

One day, we got creative in therapy. Shannon agreed to map out the different parts of her polarization and then put on her improv shoes to act out her struggle. First, we tracked the cycle of when she would use drugs and times when she tried not to use drugs in therapy (the polarization). It's almost like rewinding the game tape in sports to review what happened on the field. Through this tracking, she identified some key parts in her struggle. They were lonely, frightened, sad, shamed, and abandoned exiles, who believed they were unworthy of love due to attachment trauma in Shannon's childhood. Her husband's workaholism (his protective part) triggered the pain of those exiles. When that would happen, so would her impulse to call her dealer to buy cocaine (her firefighter), whose positive attention was to protect her from her pain of her exiles and help her feel the love she desperately longed for. If asked by her husband about her drug use, she would then lie (protective part protecting her from a shamed exile). Feeling bad about keeping a secret (exile), she would then work hard and white-knuckle (manager) not using by trying to distract herself (manager) or stay very busy (manager), hoping this would please her husband so he wouldn't leave her (protecting abandoned exile). If he left her, once again she would feel the fear of her exile's burdens of being alone, frightened, abandoned, sad, and shamed. Her firefighter who used drugs protected her from the pain of the same exiles that her manager, who tried to keep her from using drugs, protected her from. These polarized parts had two very different ideas on how to solve the problem, but neither had it quite right.

Self-energy then came to the rescue as Shannon tapped into her inner creativity, giving voice to and improvising what all these different parts inside of her wanted to say. She didn't try to think or conjure up any of these lines (that would be an analytical manager at play); she just let the creative force of her Self-energy take over.

"What did you do?" Shannon asked she walked through my door for our next session.

"I don't know," I responded. "Did I do something that upset you?"

"No," she said, "but something happened after I left last week. For the first time in fifteen years, I had no cravings for cocaine. I didn't think about it at all."

Shannon had temporarily unblended, which means that she got some space from her polarization when she creatively performed the play her inner system had written. Unblending allowed a brief shift from her chronic reactive stress response, which would trigger her addictive and impulsive firefighters to the relaxation response of extended calmness or extended access to Self-energy. Though her parts had been constantly reenacting this hardwired scene inside of her day after day, week after week, and year after year, it wasn't until Shannon gave her inner actors some love and attention (Self-energy) that they decided to take a week off. While most people don't work as creatively in session as Shannon did, anyone can access their Self-energy, which will help them intuit the messages that their parts want them to know. Some people feel their parts kinesthetically, some who are more visual see images, and others hear the notes of their inner song or the lyrics of another song that speaks for their inner system.

Shannon's break from cocaine was short, as she relapsed within a couple of weeks. In spite of that, she had enough faith to continue her connection to her Self-energy, which would allow her to also continue befriending and unblending from her parts. She committed to the process of psychotherapy. In time, she found the courage to take the next step in her therapeutic journey and get sober and save her marriage.

Color Commentary

The next step that Shannon and other people who engage in psychotherapy take to heal from the crisis of love's labor's lost, hoping to get onto the road of love's labor's won, involves some personal and historical time travel, where they go back to where it all began.

PART 3

Courage and Creative Solutions: The Road to Love's Labor's Won

CHAPTER 10

No Mud, No Lotus: Unburdening the Exile's Pain

The journey of a thousand miles begins with one step.
—Lao Tzu

No one really knows exactly when time, life, and civilization began. Many experts have some clues, though. In terms of civilization, some believe one of the first started in the Indus Valley some five thousand years ago. The Indus Valley civilization produced some of the earliest written texts known to humankind, called the Vedas, which are helpful texts when trying to understand the human condition.

Veda means "knowledge" or "to know" There were five Vedic books written during that time, called the Vedangas, which means "branches" or "limbs of knowledge." These different branches shared knowledge of language, medicine, architecture, and even the stars in the sky. One of the oldest gods worshiped in the Vedic tradition and mentioned in the Vedas is Ganesha, the elephant god. He represented new beginnings and the removal of obstacles. He still does today.

Created out of clay by Parvati, the Vedic Hindu goddess of fertility, love, and devotion, who was the consort to Lord Shiva (the god who creates, upholds, and destroys the universe), Ganesha got beheaded by Shiva when he came between him and Parvati. Feeling bad about this, Shiva replaced his head with that of an elephant and brought Ganesha back to life.

Ganesha is often depicted as part human, part elephant; he sits on a lotus blossom with four hands. One hands holds his broken tusk, which he uses to write, the other holds an axe that he uses to protect, one holds a conch shell that he can make sounds from, and the other holds a tray of sweets, for the part of him that likes to eat treats. Featured at his feet is a well-groomed mouse, eating one of those sweets. His Sanskrit name can be broken down the following way: "*gana*" means group, and "*esha*" means lord of.[xxxiv] The god of new beginnings, the removal of obstacles, and lord of the group.

The iconography and mythology associated with Ganesha has been interpreted hundreds of ways. I, as a therapist, interpret his story and the symbols he's portrayed with through a clinical lens. As the god of beginnings and lord of groups, I see the objects he holds in his four hands symbolizing some of his protective parts (protectors) in his inner system. The mouse at his foot represents one of the exiles his protective parts protects. His arms holding his protective parts are open rather than shut tight around him, suggesting that he's befriended and unblended from them. The exile (the mouse at his feet) looks happy eating his treat, which implies he's unburdened his exile's pain, as the mouse is now happy and content. He knows, as only the god of new beginnings can know, that in order to really start over, you have to grieve the past first.

That's the next step that Shannon from chapter 9 and other people take in psychotherapy that helps them recalibrate their relationship compass and map and heal their inner attachments. In IFS, we call this unburdening the exiles, whose pain is a person's inner clue for when it all began for them too.

Grieving and unburdening is a delicate process. The pain of the burdens the exiles hold in one's inner system can overwhelm and even retraumatize a person, if not unburdened with the utmost compassion and care. The key to this care is Self-energy. Clients have to have had enough of a consistent experience of their own Self-energy for them to know, beyond any shadow of a doubt, that it is a resource they really do have inside of them, not just a fluke that happened a couple of times in therapy. Just as figure skaters need to practice their inside and outside edges, crossovers, and spins, over and over again, before their body trusts that they can leap in the air and land safely on their razor-thin blades, clients need to practice, over and over again, tapping into their inner resource of Self-energy before they can take that leap down the rabbit hole and know that it is safe to meet their exiles.

Most people who struggle in the crises of love's labor's lost have a small army of protective parts, protecting a whole orphanage of exiles. While the case studies shared in this book show therapy that works with a few protectors and exiles, generally, there's more than just a few. Befriending and unblending from protectors takes time. But trusting the reliability of one's resource of Self-energy doesn't necessarily take that long at all, if one consistently practices accessing it. Once again, Ganesha offers some clues on this too.

In the Vedic and Buddhist traditions, when people pray to Ganesha, the elephant god, to help remove the obstacles in their life that keep them from manifesting their goals and dreams, they chant, *"Om Gam Ganapataye Namaha,"* 108 times daily for forty days. This takes about ten to twelve minutes a day. That number, by the way, correlates with the ancient Vedic zodiac, which followed the course of the moon around the Earth. I share this because the mind/body/spirit connection goes hand in hand with this. Before Ptolemy and the Greeks developed the twelve horoscope signs most in the West are familiar with today, the Vedics identified twenty-seven *Nakshatras*, which means "lunar mansion," based on the constellations in the sky. They then divided these mansions into four quadrants, each of which correlated to the many gods and goddesses in Vedic mythology. If you multiply 27 by 4, you get the number 108.

Considered an auspicious number, 108 has transcended time and cultures. Guess how many beads there are on the rosary or stitches on a baseball, for that matter? If you guessed 108, you'd be right. By chanting 108 times, ten minutes a day for forty days, you are consistently calling out to all the gods and goddesses in the universe to help answer your prayer. You could also view this as accessing all your inner gods and goddesses (parts) with Self-energy (chanting calms and soothes) in your "You-niverse," as well.

The Vedic tradition believes in the aphorisms "As above, so below" and "As within, so without," signaling the universe mirrors what's happening inside a person, like the golden scarab Jung wrote about, as he very much believed in the magic of the universe. In the Buddhist tradition, they believe the Buddha is inside, not outside, so magic need not apply. When someone prays to Ganesha, they are not looking for something outside of themselves to remove obstacles; rather, they are asking Ganesha for the courage (the Self-energy) to look inside themselves.

The good news is that people don't have to believe in any kind of magic in the universe or chant anything to access their Self-energy and trust that it's there. There are some excellent resources and meditation tapes available at www.selfleadership.org that can guide people more specifically on how to do that.

If they do practice connecting to their inner source of Self-energy by going inside themselves for ten minutes a day for forty days, they will soon trust, just as a figure skater does, that they will be able to take that leap and begin the process of unburdening their exiles and grieve. This is what Judy (from chapter 5), whose husband left her at midlife, did. Angry that he broke his marriage vows and left her for another woman, she quoted 1 Corinthians 13:7, saying, "Whatever happened to 'love hopes all things, endures all things'? It didn't; at least he didn't."

"No, he didn't," I said, "and it's clear how agonizing this is for you. What if, however, that passage could be interpreted differently? What if, rather than looking outside yourself, constantly reminding yourself that he left, trying to understand why he left, which is torture, what if you trusted that your inner love, Self-energy, could hope and endure all things inside of you? What if the passage is talking about self-love, rather than someone else's that you believe you need in order to heal and to feel happy?"

This spoke to Judy. Though she was raised Catholic, she didn't need any faith to find her Self-energy. She just needed to practice finding it, and she soon learned that she had what she needed to move through her grief.

Once clients begin to consistently access their inner resource of Self-energy and befriend and unblend from their protective parts, they then find the courage to go a little deeper. After some personal and historical time travel initiated by their protective parts, clients trace the story of their protectors' fears and concerns back to the beginning. Instead of falling down the rabbit hole, as Alice in Wonderland did, clients carefully and compassionately walk down the stairs to meet their exiles, with their Self-energy shining the light so they don't stumble and fall. Just as a lotus flower sits on mud and a tree has roots in the dirt, a person's exiles hide in their inner mud and roots, waiting for Self-energy to arrive and set them free.

When it does, a client can then be introduced to their young, tender, frightened, hurt, sad, lonely, abandoned, or shame-ridden exiled parts of themselves that got lost somewhere down the line. Having developed burdens and beliefs about themselves that weren't true but seemed so at the time, these parts long to be seen and heard. Judy discovered this when she tapped into an exile, a four-year-old part of her that learned the only way she could get love was to put others first. It was a belief she developed by having to endure the neglect that comes hand in hand with having a narcissistic mother. Judy then understood why she so quickly decided to drop out of school and put her dreams on hold when she found out she was pregnant. She put all her energy into raising her family while her husband followed his dreams because that is what she believed she needed to do for love.

Being held by her own Self-energy, she allowed herself to feel the pain of neglect this four-year-old part of her had been holding onto for so many years. When that happened, that exiled part unburdened its pain. With continued compassionated connected with that four-year-old part of her, that exiled part was able to develop new beliefs, such as "My wants and needs matter" and "I am loved and lovable." This was how Judy began to recalibrate her internal compass and relationship map and got through the crisis of being abandoned when her husband left, which left her now alone and starting over.

Shannon and Don healed their inner attachments as Judy did, by grieving the burdens of their exiles. They learned that the addicted parts of them that used drugs (their firefighters) came to the rescue when their exiles got triggered, either through the intimate dynamics of their partners or other work life stressors. Once those young parts of them who were stuck in the past grieved their way into the present, like Ganesha's mouse, they could start to taste and enjoy the sweeter sides of themselves and others.

When protective parts, such as addicted firefighters, compulsively do what they do, over and over again, like Groundhog Day, which was discussed in chapter 2, they are stuck in a repetition. Anyone who is struggling through a crisis of love's labor's loss is stuck in one too, reenacting their relational traumas of the exiled parts in their inner system. This is the repetition compulsion discussed in part 1. Integrating the IFS and psychodynamic models of psychotherapy, offers a systemic, step-by-step breakdown of the repetition's deeply embedded script.

Clinical Case of Jeff

Jeff came to me when his wife discovered he was having an affair. He had been married for fifteen years and until the past five years, felt satisfied in the relationship. Not sure whether or not he wanted to stay with his wife or move forward with his lover, he made the commitment to get to know his inner system and heal himself before he made that choice. After spending several sessions accessing his Self-energy and befriending his protective parts including: angry, panic and a compulsive spending part, one day, his exile appeared. He arrived to the session upset over an interaction he had with his wife. He complained that she stayed at work late again, cancelling their dinner plans that he was very much looking forward to. Feeling neglected by her, he wanted to call his lover. He came to therapy instead.

We focused on his breath and the tension he was experiencing in his body, which began to relax. As he connected to his Self-energy, his panicky part that somatically expressed itself inside of his heart, palpitated with intensity. As he befriended that part by sending Self-energy to it, it too relaxed. When panic relaxed and stepped aside, it revealed to him the exile inside of him that it protected. A memory of his three-year-old self desperately trying to wake up his father, who was passed out drunk, came forth. Jeff then discovered the frightened, sad, lonely, and abandoned exiled parts that developed inside of him due to his father's neglect. These exiles got triggered by his wife's demanding job and cluelessness about how her total absorption in her work affected him. She inadvertently triggered those exiles in his inner system, hardwired in the relational love map of his insecure attachment. As he grieved the burdens of those sad, lonely, and frightened parts, he was then able to end his affair and engage in couples counseling with his wife in an earnest way.

Clinical Case of Amanda

Amanda, who was introduced in chapter 4, was the "other" in an extramarital affair. Unattached and waiting for her lover to leave his wife, which he promised he would do many times but never did, she came to therapy in deep anguish. "Never did I think this would happen to me," she cried as she struggled with the shame she felt over her predicament. Vacillating between the extremes of hope and despair, she knew she couldn't resolve this on her own.

As Amanda got to know her inner system in therapy, exploring just as Jeff did by connecting to her Self-energy and working somatically with her protective parts, she discovered her lonely and abandoned exiles, who longed for her mother's attention. Her mother suffered from cyclical depression for most of Amanda's life, and Amanda got intermittent attunement growing up, meaning she got love and affection when her mother was well and then got neglected when her mother's depression returned. A straight A student who excelled in pretty much everything she did, she developed overachieving and perfectionistic protectors, always seeking the next best thing, that distracted her from the pain her confused and abandoned exiled parts of her felt. These exiles developed beliefs such as "A little is enough" and "Scraps are better than nothing," which she learned through the relationship she had with her mother. This was the imprinted code in Amanda's relational map that she acted out in her relationships. This made her the perfect candidate to be someone's other rather than someone's only. It was the heart of her repetition compulsion.

In time, as she found the courage to grieve the beliefs and burdens of her lonely and abandoned exiles and replace them with new beliefs such as "I'm loved and lovable" and "I deserve love and respect," Amanda was able to heal her inner attachment and develop the belief that she was worthy of more. She ended her affair and, in time, found a partner who could love her consistently.

Both Jeff and Amanda healed their inner attachments and created new relationship maps for themselves. That's how they both survived the Infidelity/Affair crisis of love's labor's lost and got onto the road of love's labor's won.

Just as there's a neuroscience involved in the creation of either a secure or insecure inner attachment and internal relationship map, there's also a neuroscience involved in grieving the burdens of the exiles of it and recreating a secure inner attachment and recalibrated compass and map. Self-energy, which some correlate with the relaxation response, helps people grieve those burdens without getting overwhelmed and retraumatized. When people engage in therapy this way, just as Judy, Jeff, and Amanda did, they are able to rewire the traumatic coding of their attachments and relational maps.

Again, this takes time, and how long depends upon the strength and ferocity of client's protective system, juxtaposed with their consistent connection with their own Self-energy that takes place both in and after therapy appointments. That's how clients can slowly remove or unblend from the protective parts that obstruct access to the exiles that need to be unburdened. Firefighters and managers will continue to do what they do and protect the exiles they protect, until there's ample evidence that it's safe not to. Self-energy is that evidence, which therapists model, session after session, through their own curious and compassionate connection with their clients.

Creating a new relationship map through psychotherapy is the creative solution that people get when they are working their way through their crisis of love's labor's lost. And that is the bait and switch I warned readers about in the introduction. The problem that led people down the path of crisis in love's labor's lost gets solved when they heal their inner attachment and create a secure inner attachment and new relationship map. That's the solution, and that's how they move onto the path of love's labor's won. Just as hope is not outside of a person, neither is the creative solution.

When someone's relationship map gets recreated, their inner compass gets reset, as well. Due north changes. Sometimes due north for clients means to stay and work things out in their relationship, as Jeff, who was having an affair, did. He realized that he was looking for his wife to take care of his neglected exiles instead of himself. He took a U-turn, stopped neglecting himself, and unburdened the pain and beliefs of his exiles that felt alone and unworthy. This allowed him to end his affair in a kind way, as he realized he was looking for his lover to take care of the parts he felt his wife wasn't. He learned that it was his job to take care of those parts himself. When he did, he no longer got so triggered by his wife's protective parts that drove her to work so much. The two of them then went to couples counseling and rediscovered the love that brought them together in the first place. They chose to marry each other all over again.

Sometimes, due north for clients means to leave, as Marilyn and Brian, who were in relationships with verbally abusive and manipulative partners, did. As they befriended and unblended from their managers who believed they needed to take care of others in order to feel secure and healed their exiles who were so terrified of being abandoned, their "Should I stay or should I go?" polarizations dissolved, as well. Leaving didn't feel so scary anymore, and they both moved out of the crisis of surviving a manipulative partner and headed onto the road of love's labor's won.

And sometimes, people who are afraid to leave a relationship because of how it will affect their children find that a creative solution can manifest outside of themselves once they recreate their relationship map inside of themselves. Lore, who wanted to be decent, engaged in couples' therapy with his wife because he wanted to do his best in his marriage and keep his family together for the sake of his children. He befriended and unblended from his protective parts, un-burdened his exiles, and consistently practiced U-turns, where he would stop looking to his wife to take care of his lonely and scared exiles and attended to them himself.

In individual therapy, he had a revelation and came to realize that the part of him that felt ambivalent about marrying her in the first place had a wisdom that he neglected to listen to prior to their nuptials. This part was not any kind of reflection on her; it was his alone to own. After he honestly did his work in therapy, he knew that staying in his marriage was hurting his soul. By healing his inner exiles who felt shame, loneliness, and the terror of ending up alone, he ended up becoming a "parts detector" himself. He understood that when his wife would guilt or shame him into staying (which in the past would always hook him back in), that that was just her firefighter, protecting her own lonely and terrified exiles. He understood that he could have compassion for his wife's parts who felt terrified of being abandoned, but it wasn't his job to rescue them or stay married for them, either. He learned that he was repeating his father's legacy of living a quiet life of desperation and decided that he didn't want his children to repeat it too. He told his wife, "I have loved you enough to do my best by you, but I don't want to stay married. I am now asking that you love me enough to let me go and model a healthy ending of us for our kids."

They uncoupled in therapy and then decided, for the sake of their children, to try something called "nesting," which was a creative solution to the concern they both had of breaking up the family. They reorganized the family instead. It's where the kids stay in their home, and the parents rotate in and out on a schedule. It worked. Lore and his wife survived the crisis of divorce, and in time, both moved onto the road of love's labor's won with other partners.

When people come to therapy in a crisis of love's labor's lost, in search of hope and a creative solution to their pain, grieving has to happen. When they do grieve and unburden the exiles' pain, new neuronal pathways, secure inner attachments with new relational maps, begin to develop. That's how they remove the obstacles that keep them from love's labor's won. More often than not, though, people stay in the crisis of love's labor's lost because they are afraid of the grief and pain. It's not an unfounded fear at all because there's nothing fun about grieving. But as Vietnamese monk Thich Nhat Hanh said, "No mud, no lotus."

The key to grieving is understanding the process better and learning how to access one's Self-energy to get it. The unknown then becomes less scary. Much has been written on grief and the stages that coincide with the process. It reminds me of a television show I watched with my father.

Feature Story: The Courage to Grieve

> Someday I'll wish upon a star and wake up
> where the clouds are far behind me.
> —Eva Cassidy, "Somewhere Over the Rainbow"

"That stunk," my father, a widower of five years as I write this, said, after we watched episode two, season three of the Starz television series *Outlander*. In case you aren't familiar with the series or books, here's the bare basics of the story:

A World War II nurse named Claire Randall reunites with her husband Frank Randall after the war ends, and they take a second honeymoon in Scotland. When visiting the countryside, they accidentally witness a pagan dance ritual around a set of stones that resemble Stonehenge, the prehistoric English monument. Mesmerized by the ritual, Claire decides to return to the site the next day, and when she touches one of the stones, she's transported two hundred years back in time. While relentlessly trying to get back to 1945, she meets Jamie Fraser, a Jacobite soldier who offers her shelter. The two end up falling in love (though she resists this for a long time, as she longs to go home), and they develop a shared mission to stop the Jacobite rebellion and infamous battle of Culloden, where close to two thousand Scotland highlanders died. Claire, who is from the future, knows what happened on the fateful day of April 16, 1746. She hopes that she and Jamie can somehow change history and spare thousands of lives. When they realize they can't, Jamie, who believes his fate is to die on the battlefield, sends Claire, who is now pregnant with their child, back through the stones to the future so that she can reunite with Frank. She does this, and she and Frank raise her and Jamie's child. Jamie, however, did not die on the battlefield that day, though Claire believes he did.

This episode, appropriately called "Surrender," captures the process of grief that both Claire and Jamie experience as they try to readjust to life without the other; it was hard to watch.

Elizabeth Kubler-Ross and David Kessler have written extensively on grief and grieving, outline five stages of the process: denial, anger, bargaining, depression, and acceptance, though the stages are seldom linear; many get touched upon and then revisited. I also view these stages as protector parts. It requires courage to surrender to the process and takes time to go through it. What my dad said at the end of that episode was right, though: it stinks.

Endings are a part of life. Whether someone dies or chooses to leave a relationship, surrendering to the grieving process is, in my view, one of the hardest things we ever have to do. Many drink to avoid it, or sleep, or shop, or eat, or smoke pot, or do drugs, or overwork, or engage in excessive sex or exercise to escape the pain. Wouldn't it be wonderful if grieving were as simple as wishing upon a star and waking up where the clouds are far behind? Unfortunately, it's not.

There is, however, a gentler way to surrender to the grief, but it takes courage to do this.

What if you took some time each day to close your eyes, follow your breath, and notice the sensations in your body? What if you tapped into your inner reservoir of self-compassion and extended it to the various parts of you that may be feeling angry, sad, lost, or lonely, or wanting things to be different? What if you honored those parts of you, listened to their cries, and allowed them to just be whatever they are, for as long as they need to be? While not fun, being in this kind of relationship with your pain will help it dissipate in an organic way.

Watching Jamie and Claire grieve each other was heartbreaking. Yet they were able to make new meaning out of their separate lives once they did. However, since this is an epic romance series, they eventually find each other again, as people sometimes do in real life. Regardless, endings always lead to new beginnings, one way or the other, as they are part of the cycle of life. Eugene O'Neill's play *The Great God Brown* describes this perfectly with the verse "Always spring comes again bearing life. Always again. Always, always forever again. Spring again, life again, summer and fall and death and peace again."

Color Commentary

Sometimes, the cycle of life, whether it be the life of a person or the life of a relationship, gets interrupted long before it feels like it should. With a lot of love, patience, time, and compassion, spring and new life will come again.

CHAPTER 11

The Redo: Why It's Never Too Late to Begin Again

> When we don't have enough dots to connect, we end up with
> very linear solutions. The broader one's understanding of
> the human experience, the better design we will have.
> —Steve Jobs

The practice of psychotherapy has transformed greatly since the time of Freud, from top down to bottom up. Early object relations theorists such as Winnicott, Klein, Mahler, and Fairbairn, who evolved from Freud, as well as attachment-oriented therapists such as Bowlby, Ainsworth, and Stern, had great insight on how the misattunements that take place during child development get imprinted early on, creating specific scripts in their relational love map, and then reenacted later on in adult relationships. Attuned therapists play with those reenactments that clients both report on in session and act out with the therapist through the misattunements that inevitably take place in therapy. Here's an example of one:

Shannon, who struggled with a cocaine addiction, had difficulty talking about her slips and relapse early on in the therapy. Having exiled parts in her system that felt abandoned and shamed, she often became angry if I asked her a question that might poke a hole in her story.

One day, she got really mad at me and said, "Are you calling me a liar?" Here, her angry protector took over as my questioning triggered her shame.

I responded, "I am not calling you anything, nor would I ever call you anything. Your story got me curious, and some things weren't clear in my mind." I then said, "And by the way, you have every right to lie to me in session if you feel the need to. I will always respect that right. I don't believe people lie because they are bad; they are just protecting themselves from the pain they will feel when they experience another's disapproving reaction."

This helped Shannon relax.

Shannon acted out with me, the fight that she has with her husband when he would question her about her drug use. Through this reenactment, she got to identify some parts in her system, particularly shame and rage, and their relationship, as well as how they hijack her system when triggered. Since I didn't yell back and threaten to leave, as her husband would, she had a corrective experience with me, which allowed her to feel safe in the therapy and become curious about what goes on inside of her.

This is a top-down approach in therapy, where clients talk about their problems; with time, and the therapist's guidance, they have their own intuitive insight, get to the bottom of things, and grieve their relational trauma. Their attuned connection with the therapist helps them create a new relational map and secure inner attachment.

As stated before, talk therapy doesn't always help clients access the implicit memories of their relationship maps, as the misattuned trauma often gets stored in parts of the brain and body, where language can't access. As Bessel van der Kolk writes in his book *The Body Keeps the Score,* trauma survivors, whether they are rape victims, survivors of war, or people with insecure attachments developed through developmental abuse or neglect, often have "no words" for their experiences. Sometimes, that's because the trauma is stored in the brain's implicit memory bank where words and language can't access, and at other times, talking about the trauma (especially when there's not enough connection to one's Self-energy) can retraumatize a person. In a bottom-up approach, which was described in the cases of Jack and Jeff, clients work from the inside first. By exploring the somatic sensations in the body, they can then identify protectors, which protect the deeper pain of the exiles held in their viscera. Working this way, rather than talking about their issues, has proven to be very effective.

IFS and other kinds of movement- or body-based therapies help clients access those implicit memories, grieve them, and then replace the learned negative beliefs with positive ones. This then creates a secure inner attachment and new relationship map. I personally favor an integrative approach between top-down psychodynamic talk therapy, as I believe clients value and grow from the clinical relationship, combined with bottom-up therapies, such as IFS, where they connect with their own Self-energy and develop a deeper relationship with themselves. And while *The Diagnostic and Statistical Manual V* doesn't list developmental trauma, or what some call complex trauma, as a bona fide diagnosis, it's been the time-proven effective working hypothesis that therapists have used from the time of Freud to today. They will continue to do so into countless tomorrows, until it gets formally acknowledged for what it is.

This book started off with Freud's seemingly impossible dilemma; he published a paper identifying trauma and abuse as the root cause of the epidemic of hysterical women in Europe. Given the number of women who came to Charcot's asylum, he realized the actual magnitude of this cultural crisis. He then caved to the pressures of the patriarchy, who denied such abuse. They did then what many perpetrators do today: deny their behavior and blame the victim. Obviously, some of Freud's exiles (perhaps one who was afraid of annihilation) got triggered; his firefighter took over, and he blamed the victims as well. He took back his paper and then said that these women imagined their abuse.

There's a technique in psychotherapy that one of my mentors shared with me, which she called a "redo." It's a creative way of healing trauma where one goes back to the traumatic event and rewrites the script to give it the nontraumatic or even heroic ending they'd prefer. My mentor attributes this technique to a therapist based out of Michigan named Michi Rose. While I am sure that what I'm about to write next doesn't adequately teach Michi's method, I'd like to use it, nonetheless, to give two historical traumas a redo. One is for Freud and the women throughout time and around the world who have endured a legacy of abuse and trauma, and the other is for Boston sports fans. Here are their better endings:

The Redo

> In case you never get a second chance: don't be afraid!
> And if you do get a second chance? You take it!
> —C. JoyBell C.

On October 25, 1986, the Boston Red Sox had a chance to end the curse of the Bambino. They were leading the New York Mets in the World Series, 3 games to 2. In the bottom of the tenth, with the score tied and two out, a ground ball rolled down the first base line. Tragedy struck.

Ten years later, in 1996, a trauma-savvy sports producer decided to give Bill Buckner and all Red Sox fans a redo. First, he showed the play where the ball went through Buckner's legs, but then instead of showing what actually happened, he played a different ending by first cutting away to footage of *I Dream of Jeannie*. With a twitch of Jeannie's nose and the sound of her theme song, magically, the ball rolled backwards. The producer then cut in footage of Buckner making that same play which he has made hundreds of times before, and viola, the Red Sox won the game. The curse had been broken, and all the Sox fans in Beantown were dancing in the streets.

I think it's time to give Freud a second chance too.

Imagine it's 1896, and Freud makes his discovery. He knows the women suffering from hysteria at Salpetriere were trauma survivors. He writes his paper *The Aetiology of Hysteria,* but just as he's about to publish it, he has a panic attack. Feeling paralyzed and polarized between not knowing what to do and needing to do something, he walks over to Angel's[xxxv] apothecary store to pick up his favorite medicine: the *Uber Coca* (cocaine). Having used it in the past to help him when he felt melancholic, he noticed that it also helped him to relax and focus. It did.

By focusing his stream of conscious thoughts, he remembers the myth of Naga Vasuki and listens to the wisdom that his panic has to offer. Realizing there could be a major fallout when he presents his findings to the patriarchal medical academy and Europe at large, he decides to wait. He realizes that he can't take this on all by himself. "Stronger together" becomes his daily mantra, and he works with other neurologists, including Joseph Breuer, Pierre Janet, and William James, to get them on board with his findings.

Appealing to their ancient mythological superhero narcissism, they all decide it's a worthy cause, and they want to go down on the right side of history. They start a small grassroots movement, slowly gathering support among physicians, attorneys, artists, and more. Within five years, Freud has a small army behind him and feels the stars beginning to align. He then publishes his paper.

It startles the world.

It's January 21, 1901, and women and men march along the cobblestone streets in Europe. Wearing their flat caps and parasols, some hold signs saying, "No More Turning a Blind Eye," "We Are Reading You the Riot Act," and more. They can be seen and heard from the mountaintops to the seashores.

A movement has begun.

The curse of misogyny begins to end, and women and men all around the globe have won their first World Series.

It would have been as if the Women's March had happened in 1896.

Feature Story: Self-Energy and the Women's March, Washington DC

They say God is in the details. Well, the Goddess is in connections.
—Gloria Steinem

The Women's March, which drew more than three million people worldwide and close to one million in DC, celebrated our interconnectedness. Triggered by hateful rhetoric in a divisive presidential campaign, this article has little to do with the politics of the January 21, 2017, event.

Rather, it is about the little moments of respectful, calm, and playful spiritedness that embodied the millions of women, men, and children on every continent of the globe who marched in support of equal rights and respectful treatment of women. It was the largest march in history, with no violence and no arrests. What made all this possible? Perhaps a phenomena called Self-energy.

The word *self* and its concept first became known to humankind some five thousand years ago, when it made its debut in the Rig Veda under the Sanskrit name Atman, which means self or soul. As a pre-Christian culture, the Vedics, who occupied what today is known as India and Pakistan, held a polytheistic worldview, where gods and goddesses of varying temperament, status, stature, and agenda worked in unison to help maintain the order of the universe. The Vedics believed that through the deities' connection to each other and their human counterparts' inner connection to them, our modern world slowly became what it is today: an amalgam of beauty, wonderment, and awe contrasted with the darker forces of nature.

Thus, was the spirit of the Women's March.

While I could list many examples of the spirit of Self-energy manifesting itself throughout the event, two events in particular blew this humble activist's mind who went to that march to protest the horrifying and hurtful words that gave way to admittedly assaultive behaviors of America's newly elected president.

The first involved the police. Yes, the men in blue have been under fire lately in the news for wrongful shootings in the United States. When a dozen or so of them rumbled into the crowd on their motorcycles with riot gear, many of us froze. They parked their bikes one by one on the sidewalk and looked toward the people, who looked back. After a long pregnant pause, one woman, with obvious trepidation, wiggled her fingers at them in a shy hello. After some delay in response, a police officer nonchalantly waved back. With the ice somewhat broken, that same woman tentatively held up her smart phone, gesturing a photo request, which was met with a "Why not?" shrug of that police officer's shoulders. She took a selfie with him, and the crowd began to chuckle. A few minutes later, countless women, men, children, and the police laughed, smiled, and posed for photos together, with some creative posturing of their bikes and ominous gear. The good vibe energy—Self-energy—dissipated the fear.

The second example involved the Metro. With roughly one million marchers in DC, the Metro was the least anticipated pleasurable experience of the event. Knowing the inevitability of being packed in like sardines, my friends and I hoped that leaving the march a bit early would somehow mitigate that. Others had the same idea, though, so no such luck. When the first overcrowded train pulled up to the landing, a couple of people squeezed their way on board. However, the majority of our crowd of strangers seemed to believe that waiting, rather than forcing our way on, would be the better option. It was. So we waited, wondering how many trains would pass us by before we could comfortably enter. It had been a very long day that required a lot of energy. Hunger and fatigue had begun to set in. Waiting, however, for what we thought would be a very long time just felt like the right thing to do.

The wait was short. Five minutes after the first train left, a completely empty train pulled up backwards on the rail, seemingly out of nowhere, destined to move forward in the direction we were heading. Excited and bewildered, we all hopped on board; most of us got to sit as we began the journey home. The relief felt nothing short of miraculous, as a part of me wondered at that moment if there really was magic in the universe.

The 2017 Women's March delivered countless celebrity speakers, huge crowds, network news coverage, uber-creative signs, and other Trumpian "best ever" factors. Much has been written about that. These two events I've mentioned probably pale in comparison to the sexier stuff of the day. But the simple, ordinary, Self-led expression of creative and compassionate connection between one human being and another, which made up the majority of this day, in my view, stole the show.

Imagine what could happen if we all did our best to allow this Self-led expression every day.

Indian activist Mahatma Gandhi said, "Be the change you want to see in the world." If more people found their inner hope and courage, as many did during the Women's March, they could be what we call in psychotherapy Self-led in the world, rather than parts driven. Here's a simple example of what that might look like:

Person A, who's in a rush (protective part/perhaps a worried firefighter) cuts off Person B in traffic (an aggressive firefighter part), and person B flips person A the bird (person B's angry firefighter, most likely triggered by a scared exile that got activated when he was cut off). Person B then gets stuck next to Person A at the next traffic light. Still angry (firefighter), Person B rolls down his window and starts yelling at Person A (aggressive firefighter), and then Person A gives Person B the finger (his aggressive firefighter who got triggered, by perhaps a scared part (exile). The two continue yelling at each other until the light turns green, and then they both floor it, trying to see who can get away first.

What if, the next time this happens, Person B, who got cut off, acknowledged his startled and angry parts, felt them in his body, and then sent the part a little Self-energy? Perhaps then, when Person B pulls up next to Person A at the traffic light, Person B looks at Person A and playfully shrugs his shoulders, signaling a nonverbal "Que pasa?" He then realizes what he did and says, "I'm so sorry. I didn't see you in the lane." Person B then says, "Okay, no problem," and the light turns green, and they both go on their merry way.

The above scenario is a lot like couples counseling. And if everyone could find a little more Self-energy within themselves, individuals would be happier, couples would be happier, people stuck in traffic would be happier, and the world really would be, in my view, a better place.

Color Commentary

When people heal themselves and create secure inner attachments, it gives them the anchor they need to continue on the road to love's labor's won, knowing that there's no such thing as smooth driving all the time. Sometimes, they will hit a pothole and lose a tire when they are on their new road or find that the pavement has ended, and they need to drive through some rough and rocky terrain for a while. Sometimes, that road is like a spiral path up the mountain, where people find themselves experiencing the same view they had when they were on the road to love's labor's lost. This time, however, they now can survive the view and, more importantly, enjoy the ride, because they can better negotiate who gets to drive, when to take turns driving, and when to take breaks at rest stops.

CHAPTER 12

Creative Repetitions: Moving on to the Road of Love's Labor's Won

Do not regret growing older. It is a privilege denied to many.
—Mark Twain

We are all living on borrowed time. Life is a gift. Love is a gift, and getting it and keeping it is not a right or a guarantee. We are not really entitled to anything, but we are free.

We are free to love. We are free to leave. We are free to return and love again. There are no wrong choices. There are simply choices. Some are driven by reactive parts of us, and some are thoughtful, reflective, and Self-led. The latter are the choices that I hope this book inspires people to make.

When people find themselves in a crisis of love's labor's lost, which most do at one point in their lives, they then have an opportunity to give themselves one of the most important gifts you can give yourself: love, self-love, that is. It can turn an insecure inner attachment to a secure one, the necessary prescription for giving and receiving love with another.

With a secure attachment and the individuated sense of self (a true self) that comes with that gift, it becomes easier to navigate the ebb and flow of two systems of messy and complicated souls filled with protectors and exiles.

I believe the gift of love boils down to something simple: It's what you do, both for yourself and your partner. It means following through on the things you say you'll do, speaking up from a Self-led place when your partner disappoints, while owning your own parts when you do feel down. The other is not responsible for your pain, just the actions they took. Once that's really understood in a partnership, when you feel wounded by the other, you give that wounded part the love and care you were expecting from the other. When that happens, when you use your own Self-energy to unburden your own pain, it relinquishes your partner from doing that. Then, the partner gets to witness it rather than take care of it, which creates a true empathic connection. When both people consistently practice this, knowing there is no such thing as perfect, then the ongoing fight they had that almost broke them apart shifts. This shift allows more safety and a deeper sense of intimacy within the couple, so that they can always begin again. The impossible dilemma now becomes a delicious dance between the two willing people, freely choosing to dance together, time and time again. "Happily ever after" becomes "Let's start again and be happy now."

Feature Story: The Year-Round Gift of the Magi

The greatest gift that's ever earned is to love and be loved in return.
—Nat King Cole

119

O. Henry's short story "The Gift of the Magi" and its many adaptations are often told during the holiday season. Though it's a story about gift giving, I think it's really a story about love, which can be told year round. My favorite version has a folksy feel and goes a little something like this:

A farmer and his wife wanted to give each other a gift. He knows that she would love a pair of golden combs to pin back her beautiful, long thick hair. She knows he would like an extra cow so he can produce more milk to sell. Neither can afford to buy their spouse their ideal gift, but unbeknownst to each other, they both came up with the same idea. They devised a secret barter plan to get each other the gift the other truly wants. She cuts and sells her long thick hair to buy him a cow, and he sells one of his cows to buy her the combs for her long thick hair.

Now, if that is not love, then I don't know what is.

As a therapist, many of my clients, both individuals and couples, come to see me about their struggles with love. "Why didn't he do that? Or why did she do this?" they complain when their wants, needs, and expectations aren't met. While there are times when the complaint is genuinely born out of one or both parties consistently not following through on what they contracted to do, more often than not, it's a different story. When I politely ask the question, "Why do you place the burden of responsibility for the other to take care of this for you?" they pause and stare at me with both curiosity and confusion. At this point, the therapy either begins or it ends.

When it begins, people start to learn that their angst is their own and not to be managed by the other. They start to look inside themselves and see what's really going on. And what that is, more often than not, is this: a reenactment of their unfinished childhood business craftily uploaded onto the other, as the unhealed wounds they carry from their unmet wants and needs incurred during childhood still bleed into adulthood, midlife, and beyond. The key here is, only they, themselves, can heal that, not the other. And if they can heal it, just by in doing it, they learn how to become relational.

That is when people can ask for what they want, what the other wants, and express their disappointments without finger-pointing and blame. That is when they can successfully negotiate their relationships and navigate their journey together, an ongoing process of new beginnings.

That is when they can love and be loved, which in my view is truly the greatest gift that's ever earned.

End Game Commentary

And there you have it: a pitch for hope, a case for courage and a book of stories, written to show you that a creative solution, which involves re-creating your relationship map and recalibrating your inner compass, is always possible. This book invites you to give it a shot. I know the stories and case studies that I shared don't have the traditional "fairy tale" happy ending. There are plenty of other books out there that do. Instead, this book shows you how to get off the roller coaster of love's labor's lost and onto the Ferris wheel of love's labor's won. Once you make that switch, then you can have intentional happy new beginnings, solo or coupled, together or apart, time and time again because that's the stuff that real is made of.

There's a verse in the Foo Fighters song *Times Like These* that beautifully speaks to the idea of new beginnings and the courage it takes to commit to having them. It says:

"I, I'm a new day rising
I'm a brand new sky to hang the stars upon tonight
I am a little divided
Do I stay or run away
And leave it all behind?"

In times like these, we really can learn to live and love again.

AFTERWORD

Memories from better days.
—Bouncing Souls

I began this book sharing my experience as an actor, training at Shakespeare & Company in Lenox, Massachusetts. I'd like to end this book, sharing an anecdote from there, as well. According to their website, "Shakespeare & Company embraces the core values of Shakespeare's work: collaboration, commitment to language, visceral experience and classical ideals, expressed with physical prowess and an embodied contemporary voice."[xxxvi] This philosophy also trickled down to their training program. Each class began with the teacher and participants sitting in a circle with a brief check-in before delving into the work. Rather than sitting traditional classroom style, with the teacher in the front and the students sitting row by row behind each other, sitting in a circle made us all part of the whole, with no one in front of or ahead of anyone else. Rather than compete against one another, we got to learn, play, and grow both from and with each other. The ritualistic check-ins before each class reinforced the idea that we all got to use our voice and say what we wanted or needed to say. No one mattered more than another. And though there was a wide range of participants who varied in experience and skill, everyone thrived there.

As I underwent the many rewrites of this book, I delved deeper into the mythology that I shared, exploring the ancestral legacies that influence today's larger cultural ecosystem in the land of love's labor's lost (at least I believe they do). The switch from a matriarchal-led egalitarian structure to a patriarchal-led hierarchical structure struck me. Gaia, the first known supreme deity and earth goddess in Greek mythology, had twelve Titan children with her consort, Uranus, the male god of the sky. Six were girls, and six were boys. When Cronos, her youngest son, killed his father and then mated with his consort Rhea, they then had six children: three girls and three boys. These six goddesses and gods made up the original pantheon of Greek mythology. In both generations, there was an equal number of woman and men, with Gaia as their matriarch.

Once Zeus killed his father, Cronos, he became the king of the gods, the patriarch who ruled Mount Olympus. His rival and Titan cousin Prometheus created the first human race, comprised exclusively of men, who allegedly were happy until Pandora, the first women created by Zeus, came into the picture. The charming and alluring Pandora, who was made of sugar and spice and everything nice, was sent as a revenge gift to Prometheus by Zeus to cause men pain and suffering, as evidenced by the evil vices that were released into the world when Pandora opened her box. Here, we see some of the first written evidence of misogyny.

How the switch from matriarchy to patriarchy (which then led to misogyny) happened, no one really knows. Much literature that perhaps could have answered those questions got forever lost when the Romans burnt the Egyptian library of Alexandria in 48 BC, during Cleopatra's reign.

Merlin Stone, author of *When God Was a Woman,* traces the roots of matriarchal societies and goddess mythology back to the upper Paleolithic time period, some ten to twelve thousand years ago.

Stone offers evidence that the roots of misogyny began during the Bronze Age (3300–1200 BC), with the rise of the Indo Aryan civilization, whose intent was to conquer other societies and subjugate them. With this, the subjugation of women and the divine feminine began as well. Polytheism still reigned, but male gods had taken a higher position above female goddesses.[xxxvii]

My takeaway from her work was that as the human race continued to evolve, it appears that the divine feminine and even the patriarchal traditions that celebrated the multiplicity of human nature slowly eroded. New monotheistic and patriarchal religions were born, cherry-picked from the wisdom of noble prophets and used for political power. God became one being who was male, and women had little place other than child-bearing, in the ever-evolving new patriarchal world order.

Those who dared defy the patriarchal monotheistic law of the land paid a heavy price, one that generally cost them their life. Heresy was punishable by death; countless women and men were burnt at the stake during the religious Crusades of the Middle Ages. It's a genocide that seldom gets acknowledged.

Today in the West, women are still paid seventy cents on the same dollar that men earn. Professions that typically attract women, such as teaching, social work, or psychotherapy, don't offer the high earning wages that male-dominated professions do. I believe this imbalance of power influences the crises of love's labor's lost that I see in my office. As for the four crises mentioned in this book (Alone and Starting Over, Manipulative/Abusive Partners, Infidelity, and Divorce), three of the four show women at the disadvantaged end of the pendulum. In consideration of the first crisis, which at the heart of the matter is human loneliness, it appears that women might be at an advantage. When considering the data compiled in James Lynch's book, *A Cry Unheard: New Insights into the Medical Consequences of Loneliness,* both sexes appeared to die prematurely due to medical conditions that have clear mind-body connections. Yet the numbers of premature deaths were significantly higher for men. I can't help but wonder if that might have something to do with the types of connections that women form with other women, which mitigate the sense of aloneness that men, who may not have those kinds of connections, experience.

When I was choosing the cover images for this book, I found pictures of a purple and multicolored elephant, which called out to me. When I shared it with my consultant, she asked me why I chose it. I told her that it reminded me of Ganesha, the Hindu god that removes obstacles. She asked me if I knew that elephant herds were matriarchal. I did not.

She then told me that elephant herds stay connected to each other and socialize with other herds. They protect and take care of each other and other animals. Sometimes, they even protect humans (provided we don't get in their way). They have empathy for their fellow elephants and other nonpredatory animals. They bury their dead and grieve the loss of them. The respect their elders; the oldest female is usually the matriarch of the clan, and when she dies, her oldest daughter takes over.

Taking care of each other and respecting elders; wouldn't it be nice if we all took a lesson from them?

Wouldn't it be nice if we lived in a world where we all took care of each other, respected the wisdom of the elderly, granted opportunities for everyone to use their voice, valued both genders and the work they do equally, which in turn might create an environment where love's labor's can win?

What if no one mattered more than anyone else and everyone got to thrive?

I not only believe that would be nice, I also believe it's possible.

All it takes is hope and courage.

GLOSSARY

Ancestral Legacy: The traditions and burdens of one's ancestors that are consciously and unconsciously passed down generation after generation.

Archetypes: A recurrent and cross-cultural symbol in mythology and art that's deeply embedded in the human psyche.

Atman: Vedic word for Self or soul.

Attachment Theory: A theory of infant / caregiver bonding that effects emotional and behavioral development of the child through adulthood.

Attunement: A world to describe how "tuned in" a caretaker is to the needs of a child and two adults in a relationship are to each other.

Befriend: Form the Internal Family Systems Model of Psychotherapy; to get to know, with care and compassion defensive parts of one's inner psychological system.

Befindlichkeit: A German expression from Martin Heidegger's *Being in Time*; meaning "being in a mood" relevant to an existential crisis.

Collective Unconscious: A Jungian term to describe a part of the mind that holds ancestral memories and archetypes.

Ecological Systems Model: Developed by psychologist Urie Bronfenbrenner, this theory identifies systems that an individual interacts with including: Individual system, System of friends, families, schools, Cultural, Political and Global systems – each effecting the other.

Ethnology: A study and science of human races and relations.

Exile: From the Internal Family System's Model of psychotherapy referring to a vulnerable and wounded part on one's inner system that is protected by other "parts".

Existential Psychotherapy: A model of psychotherapy that explores the causality of intrapsychic pain in relation to: death, freedom, personal responsibility and making meaning out of one's existence.

False Self: An inauthentic way of being with others, often to please another's wants, needs and values rather than one's own, resulting from similar experiences that a child had with their caregiver.

Feminist Psychotherapy: A model of psychotherapy that helps the client understand the political and social forces that disadvantage people, encourages an egalitarian therapeutic relationship and personal responsibility to oneself and society, while helping clients grow from their strengths.

Firefighter: From the Internal Family System's Model of psychotherapy, an extreme protective part of one's inner system that often engages is risky, dangerous or dissociative behavior to protect a more vulnerable part of the system or *exile*.

Good Enough Parenting: Refers to a child having a care taker in tuned with their needs, helping them explore the world and develop a "true self".

Hatching: A stage of infant development where the infant begins to separate and individuate, seeing themselves as separate from their caretaker. (5-9 months)

Holding Environment: A term to describe how caretakers contain and sooth a child's affect and how therapists do the same for their clients.

Implicit Memories: Unconscious memories from early childhood that often get experienced somatically.

Internal Family Systems Model of psychotherapy: A model of psychotherapy developed by Richard Schwartz asserting that all humans have an inner system of multiple parts and a healing resource of "Self-energy"

Manager: From the Internal Family System's Model of psychotherapy; a protective part of one's inner system that engages in behavior that protects more vulnerable parts of the system; *exiles* in a more socially acceptable and less risky way than *Fire Fighters*.

Miss-attunements: Refers to a lack of connection and understanding of needs between a caretaker and child or two adults in a relationship.

Object Relations: Relates to psychodynamic psychotherapy theorizing that the way adults relate to each other are shaped by their childhood experiences with their caregiver and family.

Oedipal Complex: A concept in psychoanalytic theory developed by Sigmund Freud referring to a child's unconscious desire for the opposite sex parent.

Protector: From the Internal Family Systems Model of psychotherapy; either a *manager* of *fire fighter* in one's inner psychic system that protects the *exile*.

Pleasure Principle: A concept described by Sigmund Freud that asserts human are driven to seek pleasure and avoid pain.

Projective Identification: A psychoanalytic term where one person in a relationship; parent /child, patient /therapist, or two adults; unconsciously projects parts of themselves or feelings into the other, which the other identifies with, feels and acts out behaviorally. These parts and feelings are often experienced in negative ways.

Psychoanalysis: A model of psychotherapy developed by Sigmund Freud that works with unconscious fears and conflicts.

Psychodynamic Psychotherapy: A model of psychotherapy similar to psychoanalysis which focusses on one's object relations and adult relational challenges.

Rapprochement: A stage of separation and individuation childhood development occurring between 15-24 months where a child can leave and return to their caregiver.

Repetition Compulsion: A psychological phenomena where people reenact their child hood trauma over and over again.

Self-Energy: From the Internal Family System's Model of psychotherapy; an inner resource and energetic state of calm, curious and compassionate energy that can heal one's inner system.

Separation and Individuation: A phase of infant development where and infant's identity, which was once merged with the primary caregiver, forms an individual and separate identity (0-3 years).

Somatic Psychotherapy: A model of psychotherapy which explores connections between the mind and body.

Synchronicity: A psychological concept coined by Carl Jung which acknowledges 'meaningful coincidences".

Transpersonal Psychology: A model of psychotherapy that integrates spirituality and psychology.

True Self: An authentic way of being in the world and relating to others.

U-Turn: A concept derived from couples' therapist Toni Herbine-Blank that encourages couples to take care of their own wounds rather than expecting their partner to.

Unblend: A concept from the Internal Family Systems Model of psychotherapy where a client gets psychological space from a protective part and exile.

Unburden: A concept from the Internal Family Systems Model of psychotherapy which helps the exiles in the system grieve.

Unconscious: An unknown and un-accessed part of the mind where feelings and behavior get expressed.

END NOTES

Introduction

i   Ann Sinko Level 1 Internal Family Systems (IFS) Training, 2012.

ii   "Iris." U2.

iii   Judith Herman: *Trauma and Recovery: The Aftermath of Violence from Domestic Abuse to Political Terror.* (New York: Basic Books), Chapter 1. Kindle edition.

iv   William Todd Schultz. "Why Freud and Jung Broke Up." *Psychology Today*, May 19, 2009.

Chapter 1

v   Tina Packer, Founding Artistic Director, Shakespeare & Company. Lecture and workshop on Shakespeare and Gender. Lenox, Massachusetts. 2005.

vi   Apuleus, Transalated by Joel C. Relihan. *The Tale of Cupid and Psyche.* (Cambridge, MA: Hacket Publishing Co.), 2009.

vii   Carol Gilligan and David Richards. *The Deepening Darkness: Patriarchy, Resistance and Democracy's Future.* University of Cambridge Press. 2009. Chapters 1, 2, 4, 7, 8. Kindle edition

viii   *The Age of Innocence.* Dir. Martin Scorsese. Columbia Pictures. 1993.

ix   Carol Gilligan and David Richards. *The Deepening Darkness: Patriarchy, Resistance and Democracy's Future.* (Cambridge, England: University of Cambridge Press), 2009, Chapter 8, Kindle Edition.

Chapter 2

x   Peter Buckley, MD, ed, *Essential Papers on Object Relations.* (New York: New York Univeristy Press),1986. pp-239-252

xi   Bob Fox. Object Relations Lecture. Lesley University. Cambridge, Massachusetts, 2003.

xii   Daniel Siegal. *The Developing Mind: How Relationships and the Brain Interact to Shape Who We Are.* (New York: The Guildford Press), 2009, pp-54-56.

xiii   Daniel Siegal. *The Developing Mind: How Relationships and the Brain Interact to Shape Who We Are.* (New York: The Guilford Press), 2009

xiv   Fox, 2003

xv   Buckley, *Essential Papers in Object Relations,* p122.

Chapter 3

xvi   James J. Lynch. *A Cry Unheard: New Insights into the Medical Consequences of Loneliness.* (New York: Basic Books), 2000, p. 97.

xvii   Lynch, 2000, p. 111.

xviii   "Dana". *Narcissists and Common Hoovering Techniques,* 2015. httpp**s://**www.thriveafterabuse.com.

xix   Buckley, *Essential Papers in Object Relations,*

xx   Bruce Perry. *The Boy Who Was Raised as a Dog: And Other Stories from a Child Psychiatrist's Notebook. What Traumatized Children Can Teach Us about Loss, Love and Healing.* (New York: Basic Books Publishing), 2017.

Chapter 4

xxi   Esther Perel. *The State of Affairs.* (New York: Harper Collins Publishing), 2017.

xxii   Esther Perel. Omega Institute faculty. Lector on rethinking infidelity. Omega Institute, Costa Rica, 2018.

xxiii   Perel, *The State of Affairs,* p. 49.

xxiv   *Dr. Zhivago.* Dir. David Lean. Metro-Goldwyn-Mayer. 1965.

xxv   Perel, *The State of Affairs,* pp. 37, 237.

Chapter 5

xxvi   James J.Lynch. *A Cry Unheard: New Insights into the Medical Consequences of Loneliness.* (New York: Basic Books, 2000), 89.

Chapter 7

xxvii   Kevin Osborn and Dana L. Burgess. *The Complete Idiot's Guide to Classical Mythology*. (Indianapolis: Alpha Books, 1998), p. 14.

xxviii   Osborn and Burgess, *The Complete Idiot's Guide to Classical Mythology*, p. 22.

xxix   Richard Schwartz. IFS Level One Training Manual.

xxx   Bo Forbes. Kripalu Faculty. Lecture and workshop on *Yoga for Emotional Balance*. Kripalu Center for Yoga and Health. Stockbridge, Massachusetts, 2008.

xxxi   Richard Schwartz. *Introduction to the Internal Family System's Model*. (Oak Park: Trailheads Publishing), 2001.

xxxii   Toni Herbine-Blank, Donna M. Kerpelman, and Martha Sweezy. *Intimacy from the Inside Out: Courage and Compassion in Couple Therapy.*(New York: Routledge Taylor & Francis Group, 2016), p. 19.

xxxiii   Carl Gustav Jung, Joseph Campbell. *The Portable Jung*. (New York: Viking Penguin Inc. 1971), P. 511

xxxiv   "Ganesha". Wikipedia, last modified April 18, 2018. https://en.m.wikipedia.org/wiki/Ganesha.

xxxv   Scott Oliver. "A Brief History of Freud's Love Affair with Cocaine: The Founder of Psychoanalysis Has a Serious Blow Habit." https://www.vice.com.

Afterword

xxxvi   Merlin Stone. *When God Was a Woman*. (New York: The Dial Press, 1976,) pp. 64–68.

xxxvii   Shakespeare & Company. "Company History." https://www.shakespeare.org/about/company-hisotry.

BIBLIOGRAPHY

Lynch, James J. *The Broken Heart*. New York: Basic Books, 1977.

Lynch, James J. *The Language of the Heart*. New York: Basic Books, 1985.

Van der Kolk, Bessel. *The Body Keeps the Score: Brain, Mind and Body in the Healing of Trauma*. New York: Penguin Books, 2014.

Herman, Judith. *Trauma and Recovery: The Aftermath of Violence*. New York: Basic Books, 1992.

Schultz, William Todd. "Why Freud and Jung Broke Up." *Psychology Today*, May 19, 2009. https://www.psychologytoday.com/us/blog/genius-and-madness/200905/why-freud-and-jung-broke?amp.

Gilligan, Carol, and Richards, David A. J. *The Deepening Darkness: Patriarchy, Resistance & Democracy's Future*. New York: Cambridge University Press, 2009.

Apuleius. *The Tale of Cupid and Psyche*. Translated by Relihan, Joel C: Indianapolis: Hackett Publishing Co., 2009.

Shakespeare, William. *A Midsummer's Night Dream: The Riverside Shakespeare*. Houghton Mifflin Co., 1973.

Lewis, Thomas, Amini, Fari, and Lannon, Richard. *A General Theory of Love*. New York: Random House Publishing, 2000.

Miller, Alice. *Drana of the Gifted Child.* New York: Basic Books, 1997.

Siegel, Daniel J. *The Developing Mind: How Relationships and the Brain Interact to Shape Who We Are*. New York: The Guilford Press, 2012.

Buckley, Peter. *Essential Papers on Object Relations*. New York: New York University Press, 1986.

"Dana". *Narcissists and Common Hoovering Techniques*. www.thriveafterabuse.com, 2015.

Dictionary.com. www.dictionary.com.

Schreiber, Flora Rheta. *Sybil*. New York: Grand Central Publishing, 2008.

Perry, Bruce D., and Szalavitz, Maia. *The Boy Who Was Raised as a Dog and Other Stories from a Child Psychiatrist's Notebook*. New York: Basic Books, 2017.

Schwartz, Richard C. *Introduction to the Internal Family Systems*. New York: The Guilford Press, 1995.

Schwartz, Richard C. *You Are the One You've Been Waiting For*. Center for Self Leadership, 2008.

Hendrex, Harville, and Hunt, Helen LaKelly. *Getting the Love You Want: A Guide for Couples*. New York: Holt Paperbacks, 2001.

Hendrex, Harville. *Keeping the Love You Find*. New York: Atria Books, 1993.

Mitchell, Stephen A. *Can Love Last? The Fate of Romance over Time*. New York: W.W. Norton & Co., 2003.

Perel, Esther. *Mating in Captivity: Unlocking Erotic Intelligence*. New York: Harper Collins, 2006.

Perel, Esther. *The State of Affairs: Rethinking Infidelity*. New York: Harper Collins, 2017.

Fisher, Helen. *Anatomy of Love: A Natural History of Mating, Marriage and Why We Stray*. New York: W.W. Norton & Co., 1992.

Fisher, Helen. *Why Him? Why Her? How to Find and Keep Lasting Love*. New York: Holt Paperbacks, 2010.

Osborn, Kevin, and Burgess, Dana L. *The Complete Idiot's Guide to Classical Mythology*. New York: Alpha, 2004.

Plutarch. *Plutarch: Lives of the Noble Grecians and Romans*. United Kingdom: Benediction Classics, 2015.

Wharton, Edith. *The Age of Innocence*. New York: Penguin Books, 1996.

George, Margaret. *The Memoirs of Cleopatra*. New York: St. Martin's Griffin, 1998.

Woodward Thomas, Katherine. *Conscious Uncoupling: 5 Steps to Living Happily Even After*. New York: Harmony, 2016.

Heidegger, Martin. *Being and Time: A Revised Edition of the Stambaugh Translation*. New York: State University of New York Press, 2010.

Herbine-Blank, Toni, Kerpelman, Donna M., and Sweezy, Martha. *Intimacy from the Inside Out*. New York: Routledge, 2016.

Sharp, Daryl, and Cowen, Victoria. *Pocket Jung: Pithy Excerpts from the Work of C.G. Jung with Informed Commentaries*. London. Inner City Books, 2015.

Sutton, Komilla. *The Essentials of Vedic Astrology*. United Kingdom. The Wessex Astrologer Ltd., 1999.

Kubler-Ross, Elizabeth, and Kessler, David. *On Grief and Grieving: Finding the Meaning of Grief through the Five Stages of Loss*. New York: Scribner, 2014.

The American College of Vedic Astrology. www.acvaonline.org

Easwaran, Eknath. *The Upanishads*. Tomales. Nilgiri Press, 2007.

INDEX

Y

Z